ANTIQUE HUNTING

ANTIQUE HUNTING
A Guide For Freaks and Fanciers

by Anne Gilbert

Photos by Anthony Hume

GROSSET & DUNLAP
A FILMWAYS COMPANY
Publishers • New York

Dedicated in appreciation to Don Michel, *The Chicago Daily News*—who first discovered the humorous side of antique collecting, and a new column idea.

Acknowledgments

Ruby S. Arkow; Mrs. Guy Bernard; Bernard Edwards; Mr. and Mrs. Joseph Fell; Oscar Getz; Chase Gilmore; Mrs. Ruth Jasper; Mr. and Mrs. Vern Peterson; Mrs. Walter Sobel; Leonard Weinzimmer; Chicago Art Galleries; Friends of Iolani Palace; The Art Institute of Chicago; and the Wilmette Public Library, Illinois.

The photographs are by Anthony Hume, unless otherwise noted.

Contents

List of Illustrations

Chapter 4

Chapter 5

Chapter 6

Chapter 7

Chapter 13

Chapter 14

Chapter 15

Chapter 16

List of Illustrations

1
Fancier or Freak?

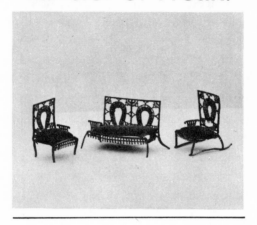

THE WHOLE ANTIQUE-COLLECTING scene is constantly
changing. The cast of characters changes radically. The
one certainty is that the entire world is preoccupied
with hunting fragments of the recent past. This book
isn't concerned with the professional, moneyed hunter
of the John Paul Getty or William Randolph Hearst
scope. Today's amateur collectors—you and I—fall
into two distinct categories: fancier and freak.

For the fancier, to whom handcraftsmanship is the
raison d'être for collecting—it is the worst of times.
There is a definite shortage of fine antique objects
made prior to 1830—and a surfeit of seekers. The

choice appears to be either to sacrifice taste and quality, pay phenomenal prices, or begin collecting Art Deco. Victorian and art nouveau have long gone into the high-priced regions. What is left for the budget collector? The only way the fancier can compete with the pros is to find new hunting preserves. Housesales, warehouses, thrift shops, flea markets, container sales—even restaurants—are selling antiques and collectibles. They are all possibilities.

Times are tough for the antique freak as well. Until his collecting habits became "in," reaching even to the kitsch category, he could hunt peacefully—and at will. Others thought he was slightly nuts to go combing junk shops and city dumps. Usually he didn't pay a cent for the pieces he now highly prizes, or very little. In fact they are so highly prized many are kept in bank vaults or office safes. Surprisingly a goodly number of hunters flip out over old insulators, barbed wire, and Dr. Pepper bottles.

Alas, today, dealers and decorators are poaching on the freaks' hunting grounds. Prices are way out for old radios, undertakers' hardware, and empty beer cans. They are all given credence with price guides and expensive hard-cover reference books. A local TV personality in Chicago pointed out that the Smithsonian now has a couple of early toasters on display. This probably started a run on tacky toasters.

There is only one thing for both fanciers and freaks to do. Learn the new rules for hunting—and the hunting grounds.

A price guide called "The Antique Trader" observes that "so-called garage and patio sales of antiques have both proliferated and degenerated to such an extent that many collectors are tending to turn away from them and back to the shops."

That offers good news for the dedicated antique hunter. With the lazy hunters beating at their doors the dealers won't have time to clutter up the house and garage sales. The lines won't be as long—and we'll have more time to examine antique and collectible possibilities. How can this be good news when we are told only junk abounds at the housesales?

If you are really serious about hunting, begin by turning off the TV and plan to give up some of those football and baseball games for the sport of antique hunting. At the public library you'll probably find several hundred recently published reference books on what you collect. Rediscover museums and restorations. Take weekend trips to see what's happening at antique shops far from home. There is no substitute for seeing and touching actual objects. How can you hunt if you don't know how to recognize the objects you covet?

For the antique fancier, instant recognition of an object, or at least "intuition," is all-important. "Mini" tours will help you to differentiate between a hand-crafted piece and a 1920's copy. You'll learn where to look for a signature on furniture, glass, etc. How to locate secret drawers.

For the freak, you'll gain new historical insights and discover new objects to search for.

The mystique surrounding the buying and selling of antiques is fast crumbling away. Not too many years ago amateur collectors were high in the economic strata. When they thought antiques, they considered nothing made after 1830—for by that time the Industrial Revolution was in full swing. Buying was simple as long as the money lasted. They merely visited their favorite antique dealer and placed an order. The whole thing was very hoity-toity. And, not much fun. It hasn't been too long since the average-income collector approached a "carriage trade" dealer with fear and trembling. The dealer sized him or her up—and treated the poor groveling creature accordingly. But, no longer. Times have really changed. The once haughty dealer is almost buddy-buddy being helpful. And, the "junk shop" dealer has become disdainful, and sometimes nasty. The reason is two-fold.

Today it is fashionable for the newly rich and the affluent young to go antique hunting on their own. The *sport is the thing.* There's something very groovy about having your friends think you have the knowledge to ferret out a rare antique—for a few dollars—on your own.

Conversely, because the freak collectors are hot on the trail of old rag-tag items, the bottom-of-the-barrel dealer is feeling important. Would you believe he can charge as much for a piece of "Depression glass" (cheap, mass-produced glassware from the 1930s) or an ashtray from the 1933 Chicago World's Fair, as another dealer charges for a fine nineteenth-century cut-glass bowl? Besides, the "fad" dealer will have customers fighting in line for that ash tray and pleading for first chance on the next one he turns up. One dealer I know began specializing in "collectibles" several years ago. Today he opens his shop when the mood hits him. He cares not that noses are pressed against his window displaying novel leaded glass windows and advertising tins. Why should he, when he knows they'll all be back whenever he opens his doors? Besides, he isn't starving. Most of his big and important pieces, like old penny arcade "girlie" machines and Tiffany shades, go to the restaurant trade or decorators for quite a stipend.

The whole antique thing is upside down. And, if you didn't know what I know, you'd give up the hunt.

Hunting these days requires *how to* bid at auctions, and haunt the least likely places. Often it's the technique that counts. A wrong move can cost you an antique or collectible.

Who cares if the dealers grumble and cry about how hard they have to work for their money. Doesn't everyone? In their desperation they often appear incognito, and try to infiltrate various collectors' societies. They have learned, and so should you, about the benefits of belonging to an Oriental Art Society or the Wedgwood Society. For practically free they have access to dedicated collectors—who pay large sums for the items they collect. How dandy for the dealer to become chummy and bide his time. Besides, he learns from the real expert collectors what to look for. Many dealers have found it is wise to go "undercover" for a while, and pretend they are either strictly collectors or "collector-dealers." This gives them a chance to be exhibitors in museum shows, and specialized antique shows. Now why would they want to do a thing like this? They get out of their original, dubious dealer category and gain a bit of status. When they go back to selling they at least appear to be a bit distinguished, and expert in their field. They can then "sell by appointment only" from their homes—and raise their prices. By now they have met "the live ones" and gained the unwary collector's confidence. As a result, the various clubs and societies try their best to screen out the dealers, dealer-collectors, or whatever you care to call them. This is why you may have a very hard time finding a like-minded group of collectors, or even getting into their group.

In spite of all these dismal practices you, the amateur hunter, do have a chance. Pay no heed to the so-called "experts" who scoff at tales of discovering a golden oak bookcase with sliding glass doors for three dollars. At this moment there is a young lawyer trying to dispose of literally walls of 1920s modular bookcases for ten dollars each. He has over a hundred legal bookcases in oak and walnut. These are the type that make good curio display cases, spice, or cookbook shelves protected from grease—or bookcases. He is simply running an ad in several papers to dispose of them. Guess what you would pay in a shop?

Many of the same hunting rules hold true when looking around in other countries or away from your local game preserve. In another part of the world it's a plus if you speak the language. However, a friend who doesn't speak a word of French managed to bargain and buy a nested-hen milkglass dish with a Vallerystahl signature. The cost was thirteen American dollars at the Paris flea market. The same covered dish is currently valued at around fifty dollars. Another intrepid hunter found good Victorian pieces going cheaper in England than in the United States. But times are changing. This may no longer be true at this reading. Hunting in other countries has an additional advantage. You may find new items with an old look in Europe that will be sold as old in the United States. Another friend brought some cheese back from Holland packaged in a green ceramic jar—a copy of the early Chinese tomb urns reproduced in the 1920s and 1930s and exported to the United States. Later, these same containers, circa 1973, showed up minus the cheese at various antique shows from ten to twenty dollars.

The wise hunter subscribes to one or more of the antiques newspapers and magazines. You'd be surprised what you can learn; and learn to avoid. At first glance you may consider investing in some of the new "limited edition" collectors' plates, bottles, jugs, jars, and junque.

Some are veddy fancy in sterling silver—with prices to match. They generally have some historical significance (but not always). As you read on, over a period of months, you come to the realization that there are nine zillion limited-edition items being made. Even the dullest bird realizes that is an awful lot of "limited editions" and "chances of a lifetime." Yet, their prices seem to go up, up, up. What to do? The best thing to do, unless you have unlimited editions of money, is to just read about them. Sooner or later they will go down in price. Down, down, and out of sight.

It is very easy to follow the trends by reading these publications. As you become a more astute hunter you discover certain objects are big in Eagle Eye, Texas— that are practically given away in Toothgap, Iowa. Suddenly, some formerly popular collectibles drop out of sight. All the commotion over an eight-hundred-piece collection of Depression glass selling at last year's Indiana auction for thousands of dollars has died down. Meanwhile, Mrs. X who bought it all has fallen on hard times. Naturally her first thought is to fall back on her great Depression glass collection. After all, time has passed—enough to make it worth twice as much as she paid. Sorry. It just ain't so. Poor Mrs. X is stuck. A victim of antique-selling propaganda. At least temporarily the bottom has fallen out of an artificially created antique market.

With plans for the U.S. Bicentennial going full blast you can bet the antique propaganda-sellers mill is grinding out hundreds of instant antiques—guaranteed to be fine investments. There are "limited editions of two hundred sterling silver Tea Caddies made in England to commemorate the Boston Tea Party and American Independence." In Britain the same thing is happening. Their Advertising Standards Authority has criticized the ads promoting these instant antiques. Princess Anne's wedding was the signal for production of gold and silver commemorative coins. Cheers for the Authority for observing that "the concept of the phrase limited edition is used too loosely. Many ads stress the investment angle without making it clear how totally dependent future values must be upon taste, world price levels and other factors—which cannot be adequately forecast by even the most knowledgeable experts."

So, gentle readers and fellow hunters, be not taken in by soft words advising you to buy this or that "as the antique of the future—an investment." The most experienced hunters buy because they like a certain type of object; wish to add it to a collection; or, because it represents the finest of handcraftsmanship. That, by the way, is part of what antique hunting is all about—an appreciation of craftsmanship often executed by hand, with unsophisticated implements.

Wherever you collect or choose to hunt—remember —all is fair in the great antique hunt. Know your adversaries and make up your rules as you go along. Are you ready?

Bottles with tiny ships inside have always been popular with collectors. Nowadays there are plenty of reproductions about and the real thing can be expensive. Try to find yours in a shop where the dealer isn't familiar with how to date old bottles. This bottle was found at an antique show for fifteen dollars, five years ago. During the nineteenth century, making ships and putting them in empty whiskey flasks was a popular pastime for sailors. It took great skill to fold the masthead down and insert the ship. Once inside, the mast was lifted and the bottle sealed.

Old Moody Pie safe found in a general store by a sharp-eyed collector. This is considered especially desirable by freaky collectors, because it has its original Moody label printed on it. At a country auction it would doubtless go for at least one hundred dollars because of its rarity. After all, there aren't too many turn-of-the-century pie cabinets in existence these days. The freaky collector can display such gems as Mickey Mouse memorabilia and ad tins behind its doors. He'd hardly use it in the kitchen for the usual kitcheny things.

English sporting prints were very big with fanciers in the 1930s. They were also quite expensive. Over the years many "restrikes" or copies were made. Originally the prints were made in the 1830s and later. The famed Henry Alken sporting-print series were bookplates when published. To find the original bookplates at a reasonable price these days isn't easy. Many have been faked with coffee stains to age them. I found this one in a society-run thrift shop for twenty-five dollars. I had first noticed it a year before, priced at seventy-five dollars. It was reduced during their once-a-year sale. It was a bargain even at seventy-five dollars. Nowadays a made-yesterday restrike can cost seventy-five dollars in a gallery.

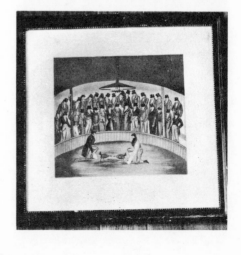

Advertising trade cards came in many shapes and sizes. Children pasted them in scrapbooks or played with them. This late Victorian trade card with interchangeable faces is a favorite with freaky collectors.

It's almost too late to get "into" Art Deco. One reason for its popular revival is an ability to mix well with antique Orientals and other carefully chosen antiques. Needless to note, it blends into contemporary settings. The stylized designs of the late 1920s are easy for hunters to spot. Colors are brash bold reds, greens, and black punctuated with silver or gold. Cubism, Indian designs, and the Ballet Russe, as well as geometric lines and elongated, sensual figures identify it. Some of the most popular Art Deco pieces caught on when the 1933 Chicago Century of Progress opened. Mass production brought out some of the worst examples. Keep in mind that the Art Deco movement affected every area of design—fashion, furniture, jewelry, even appliances. There are names like Limoges, Lalique, and Le Corbusier to look for. Leave the Art Junko for the greedy hoards. Be selective and your Art Deco will grow in value. The Art Deco pieces shown were carefully hunted down by Joseph W. Fell. They are part of an outstanding collection. The cabinet was made in Germany of pearwood in the 30s. The vase (left) from Jourdain, 1925. French bronze figure probably of Josephine Baker, 1926. Base is black ceramic ash tray. The Dutch vase (right) of frosted glass with blue and green enamel leaves, early 1920s, signed "Leuwe."

—From the Collection of Joseph W. Fell

An old tin container in "mint" condition like this one will bring over fifty dollars in a shop. This one is doubly desirable because of its bright-yellow paint finish and large size. It was found by a collector in an old store's basement.

Children's nursery rhymes and fairy tales were popular subjects for Victorian advertising trade cards. They often were used as bookmarks. Next time you see a hunter flipping through a battered book, assume he's hot on the trail of advertising trade cards. Some cards sell in shops for as much as eight dollars.

Who can resist a Victorian souvenir? This type of beadwork is often confused with the "craftwork" made by Victorian ladies during the same era. The Indian piece is backed with a shiny cotton cambric. The homemade versions used leftover materials. The beads were strung and sewed onto the paper pattern. This was then sewed to the flannel. Designs included a flower spray, leaf, or bud. The craft began with Victorians in the late 1850s. I found this one for four dollars and fifty cents. Shops have them for as high as seventy-five dollars.

Souvenir cups, with and without saucers, are considered highly collectible. This one was sold at Niagara Falls, and found in a box at a church rummage sale for seventy-five cents. You'd be apt to come across them in the freaky antique shops.

The humble revolving piano stool has come up in the world—price-wise. Ten years ago, you could haggle with a seller over paying five dollars for one in bad condition. Today they are considered collectible. The price can be from thirty-five dollars up —if you can even find one. They were originally popular from the 1890s till World War II. The earliest are most desirable; with glass-ball and metal-claw feet.

2
Preparing for the Great Housesale Hunt

BETWEEN FIVE AND seven o'clock in the morning, when the uninitiated antique hunter is snoring, the pros are up and operating.

No matter what the weather you'll find the antique dealers, junkers, and pickers waiting for the weekly early morning press shift, to walk out the doors of suburbia. Or, lurking at their neighborhood newsstand on Friday, waiting for the Saturday edition of the city papers. Or, if the Sunday classified is bigger, the same is true. This happening occurs coast to coast. The early-rising routine practically guarantees them a good running start the day of the hunt.

So important is it to grab the classified ads before the amateur even hears an alarm clock, that no sacrifice or chicanery is too great. Printers are bribed and even threatened to part with a dummy sheet, rough layout, or—hopefully—the actual paper. In fact, things are so bad that one suburban paper in the Midwest all but searches its employees on the early morning shifts. Before they leave.

The classified section is the bible of the pro—and the trail to treasures for the amateur. Consider what happens when the owner of a large home—or just an old home—moves or dies. What happens to his possessions? The answer is often to hold an estate sale. Or, to hire a professional housesale conductor. Other times the junkman is called. For this reason, some dealers are even known to follow the obituary notices. But this is not for the savvy hunter. No need to be ghoulish. Instead, be up by seven, have a cup of coffee, a dish of wheat germ and blackstrap, or whatever. This is the beginning of your well-planned, rigorous hunt. Scientific planning is smarter than hovering at the newsstand.

Map out your trail one of several ways. If you are looking for something specific, scan ads for mention of those items. Make them your first stop. Next, look under headings of conducted housesales; home furnishings; or miscellaneous. Don't look under antiques whatever you do. If a person is selling a known antique, the price will not be cheap. Unless you can't afford to pass by something for your collection, disregard these ads.

If an ad says "private housesale," to be held "tomorrow," try stopping in "today." If the "next of kin" is doing the selling, she or he will be anxious to sell— any day. The advantage is obvious. Plenty of time to sift through everything—and examine things carefully.

Ads classified "miscellaneous" can be a gold mine—

or a sand pit. Dealers don't like to waste their time on such unknown quantities. However, the amateur may be lucky. That old Victorian bird cage may be just what you are looking for.

How well I remember one housesale, just down the block from my home. The sale of the "deceased's" belongings had been in progress three hours before a neighbor told me about it. The next of kin were handling the sale. It looked most promising. The foliage had crept well up around the old Victorian frame house. As I charged in the front door I ran smack into a well-known dealer carrying out two handsome clocks. One a Willard, the other a Seth Thomas. Inside, sold signs were on every piece of Eastlake Victorian furniture, and only a few pieces of broken crockery remained on the "sold" dining table. Rather than waste time going upstairs I charged into the basement. It looked like the bones had been picked clean. Still, I wondered, had anyone climbed back of the old coal furnace? I could barely make out objects in crumbling newspapers and brown paper. Fortunately, I had my flashlight in my shoulder bag. And, I was wearing old jeans. Groping about I dislodged eight packages, and a couple of others were too far back to reach. Luckily for me, the little girl from next door was right behind me. "I'll climb in there," she said, scurrying up like a little mouse. She handed out one of the most charming bird cages I've seen. It looked like a small wooden gazebo in need of a good rain. The other wrapped packages contained— eight brass bird cages. They were late nineteenth century, and very delicately made. My little friend and I dashed to the cash line to ask the price. "Oh, take the lot of them for a dollar," laughed the cash lady. Her husband, who was helping out, just shook his head. "You should have got here earlier. The stuff is all gone now.

Except there's one high kitchen cupboard I ain't opened yet." I practically handed him the ladder. He laughed so hard at my eagerness he almost fell off. "Now what do you suppose is in here," he said, prolonging the suspense.

He handed down a dusty, greasy, leaded-glass shade of many colors. "You can have this for five dollars." While it wasn't a signed Tiffany, it was a beautiful shade. I later gave it to a creative friend as a Christmas gift. She turned it into a smashing lamp. The bird cages were sold at a later garage sale for two dollars apiece. Later they turned up for ten dollars in a local shop. The girl next door kept hers and painted it bright yellow.

Another approach assumes that you don't have a chance against the pros at the professionally conducted housesales. Since the early birds will have first chance at the obvious items of value, you should purposely be either late or early. If you plan on early—be there one hour or more before listed sale time. The large conducted housesales use a number system. Thus, dealers (and you) can go early, get a number and go have a cup of tea somewhere till "show time." The poor souls who are waiting in line when you arrive, relaxed, one hour later, will be allowed to enter only after the number holders. If you are going to be late— make it ten minutes before closing time. Your only chance is to discover some things the others have over-looked. Try it both ways just for variety.

After you have mapped the trail, check your equip-ment. Now what hunter wouldn't go fully equipped to the chase? A small, strong magnifying glass is a must. How else are you going to see quickly if a piece of silver has a hallmark or if that Coca-Cola tray says "Made in Japan"? A small magnet is equally vital for ascertaining metals. Is it really brass under that painted candle-holder or lantern? Is the hardware iron or brass? Looking for old Sandwich-type glass, you'll want to tap gently. The magnet will do. If the glass rings, chances are it's at least an antique. You'll also need a measuring tape, if you happen upon old window shutters or bookcases. Otherwise, while you go home to look for a measuring tape, someone else will already have removed them from the premises.

Sometimes it's wise to bring a small 60-watt light bulb. Old garages, attics, and basements generally have burned-out bulbs. If you can't see, how can you discover a case of old bottles in the coal bin?

Clothing is of course a matter of preference. While it is a bit dangerous to wear spiked football shoes, there is common sense behind such thinking. I've noticed that most battle-toughened pros wear sneakers, jeans, and caps or head coverings. Climbing into dirty rafters just isn't practical in high heels and suede slacks. That's how you separate the dedicated from the just-lookers.

Don't snicker at the mention of a first-aid kit stored in the car. A bloody nose, scratched shins, and lumps on the head are common casualties. Of course, if you faint easily, this could be serious. You'd better believe that the thundering herd of hunters stops for nothing— not even a hunting casualty.

I still shudder to remember an early conducted house-sale at a suburban mansion. The line curled around the house and three police squad cars were parked at intervals. I imagined they were armed with Mace. As the doors swung open and the pros surged forward a crash and scream were heard. A tiny blonde (but tough) picker was fighting over a Regency chair with a hulking, three-hundred-pound dealer. She kicked him in the shins, seized the chair, and dragged it to the cash desk. Recovering from his wound he attempted to salvage his find. No use. By then the frantic housesale conductor had the girl's money in her hand. "Please, let's be ladies and gentlemen," she pleaded. But who could hear above the arguing? That dealer should have worn shin guards.

What is it really like at most conducted housesales? Picture a bitter cold, windy, Saturday, January morning in front of a 22-room Victorian house. A crowd of over two hundred is lined up. More cars arrive every moment. The people in line are a variety of types from affluent to second-hand shop owners. They concentrate on the front door. Periodically, it opens and one of the sale conductors yells out, "Anyone else need a number?"

When the door finally opens and the numbers are called this diverse group will join together in the active sport of hunting antiques and collectibles. Tension mounts. What is waiting behind those doors—besides the housesale personnel and their cash boxes? Here are fathers who have been dragged from their Saturday newspapers. Young mothers juggle snotty-nosed, whimpering babies in their arms. (Some sales forbid any child under thirteen.) Young men in pony tails and jeans shift uncomfortably, trying to keep warm. Well-to-do matrons in mink-lined denim jackets and Gucci pants mumble impatiently to each other. And, at the head of the line are the dealers, junkers, and pickers.

After attending a few of these sales you'll soon recognize many of the faces. Being observant of the competition is most important. You'll know what they look for and their buying techniques. You'll also know how they overcharge when you come across their purchases in their shops. And, you'll learn to leave your good manners home.

Dedicated hunters don't go with friends. It is a good place to lose them. Or, if you do take a friend, be prepared to give up a discovery to him—if he claims he saw it first. You'd be amazed at how quickly friendship disintegrates in the heat of the chase—should you both corner the same quarry.

It happened to me once. A friend and I discovered an old hand farm tool in the rafters of a garage, perfect for a garden ornament, entwined with ivy. As I handed it down from the rafters, my friend proclaimed it was hers. Should I argue? Now if we go together, I head for the opposite corners.

Let's see who hunts at the housesale. One of the first to arrive is Max the Picker. Once inside he moves like a hound on the scent—from object to object—grabbing and snarling. He has a package of "sold" labels that he slaps on almost everything in sight. He hopes to beat the legitimate dealers to choice objects—or what he thinks is salable. He then sells his finds to other dealers and flea-market entrepreneurs. As of late he has been stalking the nostalgia collectibles.

There are no smiling, happy faces among the pros. To them, and rightly so, this is a serious business. They aren't happy that the amateurs are on the scent. They have to really work fast to make a dollar these days. You don't see the carriage-trade "gallery" owners here. They rely on Max the Picker to score. Or, they come incognito. They are still, on the whole, in another antiquing world. Auction galleries are usually their haunt.

Harriet the Junker and her elderly husband are breathing hard, waiting for their number. Their quest is slightly different. In the basement of their home-shop, Harriet's husband repairs and refinishes most of their purchases. A broken chair here; a table with a leaf missing. The housesales have made serious inroads into their livelihood. They haven't culled much lately and those who have shopped in their basement inform me prices were higher than ever. They are quite surly about the whole thing.

The Hotfinger family is here, too. Mother, grandfather, and sister. This trio buys a little and "lifts" a lot. Should you find yourself squashed between them in the line, check your pockets. By now everybody (regulars, that is) knows them. They are one of the dangers the antique hunter must be prepared to meet. You'll find more about them later on if you try to sell any of your things.

One of the most dangerous adversaries is Baby Doll. She is a petite blonde who swings a mean karate chop. Generally she wears tailormade recycled denims and lots of handmade silver jewelry. Remember her. She's the one who gave the sore shins to another dealer, and made off with the trophy. She claims not to be a dealer, but a collector. Of course she sends a few little shipments to her cousin the dealer in a nearby city.

Meanwhile, as you shiver in line, you begin to get depressed. What chance do you have with two hundred people ahead of you? For one thing, use the time spent waiting to advantage. Notice what people are carrying out. There goes Max the Picker with two seedy Oriental rugs, a moosehead, and a small wooden icebox. The junkers leave with Victorian side chairs in need of caning, and leaded-glass windows with broken panes. This isn't to say they haven't purchased other things to carry out one-by-one. Some file out carrying bales of wire, clothes, boxes of kitchen china and books. The Hotfinger family, looking suspiciously bulkier than when they went in, stagger out with a tired mink stole, boxes of costume jewelry, a rocking chair, and a copper boiler. There is a murmur from the crowd as Baby Doll wheels out an old baby buggy filled with a silver candelabra and soapstone lamps. No telling how many dealers are writhing inside with battle scars. At least you know the type of things that are or were inside. Or, do you?

When you begin to feel there is absolutely nothing left in that old house, you are pushed through the door by the pulsating crowd. This is the moment of decision for the hunter. Which direction should he go in? Straight ahead is a room filled with books and antique silver—and a line of people waiting to enter, five at a time. To your right is the living room. People are nose-to-nose, pushing, shoving, grabbing. The first floor is out. To the left are the stairs, leading to bedrooms and the attic. Traffic is heavy. You can hear the sounds of conflict from where you stand. That leaves you with two choices—the basement or the attic. Ready! Set! Go!

Hunter's Tip: Go first to the least popular room. It is just good sense to leave the silver room alone in this instance. Either the items are too high priced to be bargains—or all of the good pieces have been bought. In any case standing in line is a time waster. Where should you go?

Beware Moonlight Madness Mystique . . . the Downfall of Many a Stalwart Hunter

This rather new approach to conducted housesales holds a preview sale the evening before the two regular sale days. There are two very good reasons for this:

1. The hunter feels in his subconscious mind that he is personally being invited to buy priceless antiques and collectibles before other hunters. To the benefit of the professional housesale conductor the hunters, lured by this exotic scent, come in droves.

2. By holding the sale at night the hunter's resistance will be lowered. After all, he or she has been either working at a regular job during the day— or going to other housesales.

It begins innocently enough with a full-column newspaper ad. See if you could resist!

Quantity and Quality
Antiques and Collectibles
54 Turpentine Drive, Gangrine Village
Thurs. Night Preview—8 P.M.–10 P.M.
Saturday, Jan. 24—10–4 P.M.

Gangrine Village one-owner home (built 1905)—nothing ever tossed out. Be prepared to spend time and bring trucks, boxes, bags for packing your treasures.

In the library extraordinary collection of Spanish American War books, maps, handwritten diaries (written on the battlefields) and hundreds of other books; also medals, ribbons, and children's books. Most in fine condition. Rare coins. Fine linens and laces, most never used. Postcards, antique toys, Christmas items, handpainted china, silver, Rookwood, American Indian bowl, Victorian clothes, kitchenware. Political buttons, antique paintings, wicker chairs, Victorian music cabinet, Antique Oriental rugs, and much, much more.

Golden Daze Sales

Are you ready to rent a panel truck and take off?

It is preview night, the moon is full and the suburban dogs are howling. *One hour* before the designated time you drive up. Already there are no parking spaces for two square blocks. Undaunted you march to the towering brick house, blazing with lights from basement to third-floor attic. The wide stairway is filled with other hunters pawing and snorting with anticipation—and cold. It is January in a Midwestern suburb. Then you discover numbers are being given out. They are already up to two hundred and doors don't open for forty-five minutes. Trying desperately to squeeze in and up toward the giver of numbers, you finally have a ticket thrust in your upheld hand. You are lucky to have your hand. Others are also grabbing. You recognize many of the familiar dealer faces in the light of the moon. Shoulders hunched they wait unsmiling for the initial starting bell. The doors open and the first fifty charge through. You and the others wait to see what they bring out. After what seems endless time ten people leave.

"A nothing sale," says one.

Another comes out with an angel food cake tin. A third pushes her way through holding on high—a lace crowned hat from the 1930s. "What did you pay?" someone asks.

"Five bucks," she replied.

"This was the big one, baby," smirks one carrying a rolled Oriental rug. "Twelve hundred bucks and a bargain."

"So we'll get three thousand for it," smiles his partner.

Finally your number is called. You head first for the living room, to see the oil paintings and Oriental rugs. Most of the furniture has been pushed against the wall with sold signs on it. The remaining rugs, priced at nine hundred, five hundred and three hundred, are threadbare and pretty ugly. The oil painting remaining is priced at four hundred and a real dog at any price. Your next thought is the library. However, there is an usher-guard at the door—and another long line. People in the library are flipping through books and stuffing them into shopping bags. From what you can see these are strictly rummage sale books at antique store prices. Next you charge up to the second floor. Perhaps there is a small desk, night stand, or chair? Yes indeedy and just waiting for some desperate hunter who feels he'll never be able to find another antique. An ungainly Empire chest with heavy bowed scrolled pillars is priced at one hundred and fifty dollars. A late Victorian side chair with a broken cane seat is four dollars. Racks of clothes from the 1900s dangle limply from hangers. In each room is a guard-usher saying "don't handle the merchandise." For a moment you think you are in the designer shop at a posh store. Fussy, fussy at a house-sale? You stop your frenzied searching and watch the others. You note they are in the throes of hunters' moonlight madness. They are grabbing and buying everything in sight without even giving it a second thought.

Only the kitchen, dining room, and library are left. The attic and basement will be saved for another sale, you are told.

In the kitchen there are a couple of graniteware coffeepots for five dollars each. And, lots of greasy baking tins. The dining room has cut-glass nappies (small relish dishes with a handle) at twenty dollars apiece and a decanter without a stopper for forty dollars. Several pieces of pink Depression glass are being fought over at five dollars and up each.

As you turn to leave one of the ushers gives you a suspicious stare. "You didn't buy anything?" You feel you should empty the contents of your handbag or go under an X-ray. Brave hunter that you are you didn't succumb to the lure of the moonlight housesale. Outside numbers are still being called and the line is only half as long.

Hunter's Tip: Unless you are only looking for a vicarious experience skip the moonlight preview conducted housesales. Prices are super high and the quality of merchandise is super low. You can believe anything worthwhile has gone to a few dealers the day before.

Anne Gilbert

When a housesale is this well organized with numbers, ushers, guards, and the antiques are overpriced for what is offered—it is a hunter's trap. If a housesale is more expensive than a dealer's prices why waste your time?

While you can't always judge a good hunting spot by its exterior, this old house looks like a good bet. It practically oozes age from every creaking stair-tred. It did indeed turn out to be good hunting with everything from an old metal ice cooler and trade cards to handmade French lace collars and Victorian furniture. The dealers were first in line to look a little and buy a little. Many put closed bids on objects they will hopefully pick up after the sale, at reduced prices.

Housesale organizers of the new breed often have cutesy names like Ladies Three, Aunti-Q, and The Hobnails. Others of long standing use their own names as a mark of status and dignity, such as Hazel Ann Stupple. These old timers often refuse to conduct the affair unless there is a guaranteed sale of at least six hundred dollars.

Antiques' popularity runs in streaks. One year "everybody" buys Carnival glass. A couple of years ago everybody (meaning dealers) was hot after *Flow-blue* ironstone, like this pattern. As you probably know, it is so-named because the printed designs have a smeared effect. This was caused by the cobalt coloring flowing from the design onto the plate. Some pieces are heavily smeared and dark; others have clearer designs. Now that the fever has died down, the serious hunter once again can pick up a piece here and there for a quarter and up at garage sales.

Basements yield some fantastic finds, along with old moldy clothes and baby bottles. At this one, the shopper in the picture found an early pressed-glass cruet for one dollar and some postcards of the Columbian Exposition of 1893 for a dime per set of four.

Hunters have a good chance of finding old valentines at the big housesales. While the dealers are busy grabbing the cut glass and Carnival glass, you can leisurely flip through boxes of old letters and old books. Often the seller will be taken by surprise and let you have the valentine for a quarter. Not bad when you consider they go for twelve dollars and up in some shops. Even worse, many of the Prang valentines have been reproduced—especially the little decal hearts and cupids. So, unless you find it yourself, it's hard to know what you are getting.

Dainty Victorian chairs are hard to come by for twenty-five dollars. This one was lying in a basement corner when found in sad shape. A piece of the back was missing and the stuffing was coming out of the seat. If it had been in good shape and on view in the living room you can bet it would have been snapped up for fifty dollars. At least a similar chair, in good shape, was so priced at the same conducted housesale. By looking around in the basement I found the missing piece. A good furniture glue and a home upholstery job put my purchase in working order.

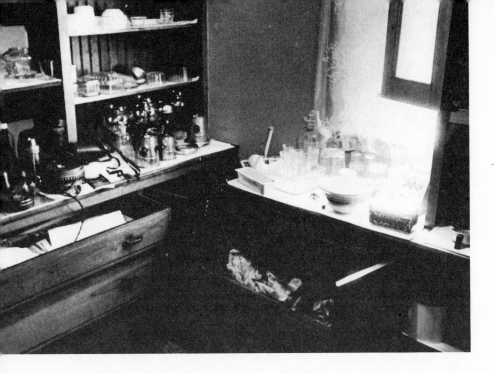

Inside the pantry it's a hunter's heaven. Old bottles, pottery, and even some woodenware turned up. Brave hunter that you are, you leave your manners home and plow right into those open drawers. Never let a little mess deter you.

A tiny teenager scrambled into an equally small basement crawl space to rescue this charming wooden Victorian bird cage. While she was groping about, she discovered dozens of small brass cages. We split them between us, paying a quarter apiece to the amazed seller. The owner had raised birds and never thrown away any of the cages. Later, the cages were sold at our neighborhood garage sale for two dollars each. Still later, we spotted them in a dealer's window for ten dollars. The youngster kept the wooden cage (pictured), and sprayed it bright yellow for use as a planter. This sale, held in an old Victorian frame house, was deluged with dealers before the sale day. By the time I arrived it had been plucked clean—but for the bird cages and a couple of other unusual items mentioned elsewhere in the book.

—*Courtesy*: Joan Jasper

Cut glass is high on dealer priority. For a while it seemed every antique shop was stuffed with cut glass. Prices for a small dish, finely cut, and in mint condition ranged from fifteen dollars up. A signed piece always seems to have a higher price tag, even though it doesn't mean the cutting is better than on an unsigned piece. Usually all the cut glass is in a room with the silver at the conducted housesales. Unfortunately housesale prices on glassware are almost on par with shop prices. This means the dealers have to, in turn, raise their prices. Usually they try to get the seller to knock down the price during the final sale hours. Unless it is too highly priced, it will be sold right away to the amateur hunter who knows a good buy when he sees one. This four-inch cut-glass dish, unsigned, was purchased at a conducted housesale for eight dollars —only because I peeked through the housesale window in advance and spotted it on a dining table. By heading directly for it I was able to beat the dealers.

The house with all the bird cages had a few other hidden treasures the dealers didn't spot. The owner and seller thought it was so amusing that I was buying his grandmother's bird cages that he jokingly mentioned crawling up into a top kitchen cabinet: since he claimed he had forgotten to clean it out, it certainly promised at least a surprise. So, out of the goodness of his heart, he himself climbed a ladder to the top cabinet. He removed just one object—a multicolored, leaded-glass lamp shade. He couldn't stop laughing as he sold it to me for five dollars. It wasn't a Tiffany, but it is a beauty. I gave it to a friend for Christmas. She had it made into this handsome lamp.

3

Beginners' Luck at Housesales

THE FIRST HOUSESALE I ever went to was my own. A sale to dispose of the effects of my late mother-in-law. If you had been there, you might have bought an authentic Louis XVI *secretaire à abattant* for one hundred and fifty dollars or a Regency game table for twenty-five dollars.

If that sounds totally incredible you have to realize that this was fourteen years ago when the general public wasn't "into collecting." My interests at that time were limited to old bottles and early American pressed glass. Antique furniture was far beyond the reach of a young married's purse—at least mine. The only antique furniture I owned was an Empire sideboard rescued from an apartment-building basement.

Since my mother-in-law had loved antiques she had begged us not to dispose of the *secretaire*. She had purchased it in France around 1927 for fifteen hundred dollars and insisted it was very valuable.

Even fourteen years ago there were professionally conducted housesales. Generally they were conducted only for the very wealthy. My mother-in-law had gone to many and had once suggested her things should be sold this way. The few housesale ladies in existence were very fussy about who came to their sales. They maintained mailing lists of tried-and-true customers, dealers, and auction houses. It had been a source of pride to my mother-in-law that she was on a couple of the mailing lists.

Rather timidly I contacted a Mrs. B. regarding a sale. She agreed to come over and price the items and then send out a mailer. It was most disappointing when she told me I couldn't get more for the *secretaire* than one hundred and fifty dollars and should price it accordingly. Now I'll admit the secret panel back of the pigeonholes did get stuck, and some of the veneered border had come off. But, still and all it stood a commanding piece, five feet high. Neo-classic figures cut from tiny pieces of veneer decorated the drop front and the bottom doors. It still had its original quaint key. It was supposed to be very old, but how *old* was old?

When a family is in a state of grief they rely on the opinions of friends, relatives, and business associates. The first inclination is to get rid of everything. This is how housesale discoveries are made. The sellers often don't know the true value of objects—and more often could not care less. The overall sum of money is more important than whether an individual piece is a priceless heirloom. So it was with our housesale.

What I didn't know was that my mother-in-law had bought many expensive reproductions. On the bed headboard was the name of a fine furniture store—not a French cabinetmaker's signature. The same appeared on the Regency-style sofa, French Provincial chest, and bedroom furniture. I didn't know you were supposed to look for labels. But, the housesale lady and the potential buyers did. At this point most of the furniture jumped from considered-antique to secondhand furniture. At my insistence the housesale ladies placed a three hundred dollar price on the *secretaire.* The stipulation was if it didn't sell on the first day the price would be reduced to one hundred and fifty dollars. Sadly I agreed. There were bills to pay.

Cut glass, Godey fashion prints, rugs, and china were completely sold out in the first hour. The dealers, I was told, had come first. Over fifty, according to Mrs. B.

The *secretaire* was reduced to one hundred and fifty dollars. Mrs. B. told me none of the dealers thought they could sell it. Not even a certain Mr. G. who was very high priced, or one of the pickers for a fine auction house. Why had they passed it by?

The second day over two hundred people walked through the apartment doors. One young woman bought the game table for twenty-five dollars, declaring she was going to cut the legs down and paint it to match her modern chairs. Most everything had been sold by closing time—four o'clock. The *secretaire* stood alone in the midst of newspapers, boxes, and the empty living room. Our total proceeds, after paying the housesale people, were three hundred and fifty dollars.

It cost ten dollars to move the *secretaire* to our kitchenette apartment. My husband suggested we call in one of the better antique dealer-appraisers ourselves. For twenty-five dollars we could have the piece appraised and perhaps the dealer would then buy it? How naïve can you be?

The dashing Colonel M. made his pronouncement on

my *secretaire.* It was "a piece of the period." What period? "Oh, it is definitely French and late eighteenth century. In its present condition it is worth around four hundred and fifty dollars. But, I'll buy it from you for two hundred. It will cost a bit to restore, you know."

Somehow I managed to resist this magnanimous offer. Instead I went to the public library and began researching French furniture. You'd be surprised how much you can learn if you are willing to spend the time. I learned among other things that identifying authentic antique furniture takes a lot of patience. It is almost like taking it apart piece-by-piece visually. Is the leg right, is the wood right? Could the hardware have been replaced with newer pieces? Was there a signature? If so where do you look for it?

More important, I learned that the only way to be sure of authenticity was to know as much as I could about what I hoped to collect.

Fourteen years have passed since I almost sold that *secretaire* for one hundred and fifty dollars. I am still at a loss to understand why not one buyer was even vaguely interested in it. Perhaps this is why I don't believe that a young, beginning hunter has to settle for just any near-antique or fad collectible. Sure, people are more antique-minded these days. But, they are generally not research-minded. To see and compare a hand-crafted chest with a bulky machine-made one is an education. If you don't know what a Hepplewhite or American primitive chair or chest looks like, how will you recognize one at a housesale? If it is disguised by paint and new hardware the job is well-nigh impossible.

Beginning Hunter's Tip: You can't know everything immediately about every antique. You have two choices. Take your chances on a piece that may have some of the features you recognize—if you don't have to pay more than five dollars. Or, specialize in one period and learn as much about its characteristics as possible.

Many types of sales fall into the housesale category. There are private or conducted housesales; estate sales, porch sales, garage sales and backyard sales. The beginning hunter should try his luck at all varieties. There is really no way to tell which is going to turn up a worthwhile collectible or valuable antique.

Not until six years ago did I begin seriously hunting antiques anyplace but shops and shows. Once in a while when a friend of my mother's would go into a convalescent home, I would have a chance to go through her things before the dealers were called in. This is really the best way to buy at a housesale. The "family" generally takes their selection first. Just like my housesale years ago, the relatives just want to get rid of the things. Get over your initial feeling of sadness at going through someone's personal effects. If you are going to be an antique hunter of merit you'll have to become battle-hardened. Think of it all as saving worthwhile objects from being destroyed or given to the junkman.

During my early housesale hunts I was so tenderhearted that I could hardly flip through the boxes of old letters looking for valentines or unusual postcards. It seemed ghoulish. Now, it's adventurous. Gradually it dawned on me I could furnish my home inexpensively and with individuality by shopping the housesales. I learned to open drawers and doors, to tap glass, and crawl in dirty attics.

An elderly upholsterer ran a small advertisement in a suburban paper. Yard goods, supplies, and some furnishings were mentioned. Quite by chance two friends knew him, and felt there might be some antiques. His shop was in an old Victorian house. He was in his seventies, and had bought out another upholsterer some forty

years ago. With his purchase came the other upholsterer's furnishings and supplies.

By the time we arrived there were sold signs on the
marble-top washstand, round dining table, and most
everything else in sight.

"What about the basement?" I asked.

Reluctantly he led us down the rickety stairs. A single
dim bulb lit the room. As my eyes grew accustomed to
the dark I made out piles of lumber, some cabinets, and
lots of upholsterers' equipment.

One of my friends attacked a pile of lumber with
vigor. "Help me, I've found something," she urged.
Bit by bit we uncovered a "davenport" desk. We cursed
ourselves for having no flashlight. "How much?" she
asked. He scratched his head. "Ten dollars?" he questioned. In no time at all, we were flipping old boards
aside. I pulled out a table in two pieces. One of the
metal animal-paw feet had caught my eye. It was an
Empire mahogany game table in fairly good shape.
"You can have that for five dollars," said the upholsterer.
"Lots of this stuff belonged to the other man. I haven't
looked at it since I bought the place."

A library table, several country chairs, and mirrors
were claimed by my two friends for a couple of dollars
each. Two bentwood chairs were mine for ten dollars.
Just as we were about to leave I noticed a work chest
against the wall. The white porcelain knobs shone
through their dust and dirt. It had at least thirty-six
drawers, and one missing. It was stained with glue and
painted a dark, peeling brown. A smell of mold ema-
nated from the damp wood.

"Oh, you don't want that thing," laughed my friends.
"It's a mess."

"Take it away for nothing. It's yours," chuckled the
old upholsterer. "I just hope it doesn't fall apart before
you get it out of here."

With help from husband and friends the multi-drawered chest was removed to my garage. I took all the drawers out and hosed down the entire piece. I even set it in the sun hoping to get rid of that moldy smell before I set about removing the layers of paint. I left it there overnight. I had failed to notice the pieces of paper washed out till the following day. Among the debris was a Confederate one-hundred-dollar bill from Louisiana. More surprises were in store for me. With the old finish removed the piece was a mellow, golden pine. It had been made by hand. One of the knobs was a wooden mushroom type, suggesting possibly that the porcelain ones were added later. For a while I used it as a serving bar at parties, topped with a brass fender and tiles.

The Empire game table responded to some "feeder" polish and brass polish. It is great for everything from games to an extra serving table.

Hunter's Tip: Don't despair if you arrive at a sale late to find things marked sold. Inquire if you can go into the basement, garage, or attic. Take a light bulb or flashlight and even a pair of garden gloves. Dig in!

Wonderful things await the basement hunter, providing he or she is nosey. A friend alerted me to the second day of a basement sale in a very ordinary brick bungalow around the block. "There's one of those glass chicken dishes you collect," she said. "It's only a dollar."

The chicken dish was a recent reproduction. Most of the tables were laden with clothes, books, and odds and ends of kitchenware and glass. As I turned to go I glanced absentmindedly at the washtubs by the door. A huge sponge was covering some kind of cup. The handle caught my attention. It was all I could see, but it was white with a scroll twist. Could it be something Victorian? Under the sponge was an occupational shaving mug of a gymnast.

"Do you want to sell this?" I asked.

"Oh, that dirty cup! I just found it in one of the boxes yesterday," exclaimed the seller. "Is two dollars too much?" she questioned.

Now at this point in time I knew zilch about shaving mugs except that people collected them. I thought it was probably worth about ten dollars at most.

Hunter's Tip: When buying an unpriced item at a private sale, always ask the seller to make a definite price. Sometimes this is hard to do, and you will have to decide on a fair price. Yield not to temptation to gyp the seller. However, keep in mind the seller would only toss the article out and the junkman would get it free.

As it happened the shaving mug was worth over one hundred dollars.

That basement yielded quite a few hunting trophies.

"Are there any boxes you haven't gone through yet?" I asked the seller. She led me back into a cubicle with not only boxes but bushel baskets stuffed with paper-wrapped objects.

"Why don't you go through it? If you see anything you like and I don't want it you can make me an offer," she said.

Three hours later I had come up with an R. S. Prussia hatpin holder, a cocoa set in cabbage-rose pattern, an Indian basket, a Victorian baby cup, and at least a dozen antique odds and ends. The woman felt I had done her a favor and was glad to get rid of the whole mess for five dollars. "I couldn't take a cent more," she said.

A couple of years ago I dashed breathlessly to a sale advertised to be in the oldest house in the area. The sight of sold signs told me the dealers had been there before me. One thing they had overlooked—probably purposely—was a seven-foot mahogany Empire bookcase desk. It was pretty ugly with its animal feet and peeling veneer. Several of the glass knobs were missing. Just right for my typewriter and reference books though. The price tag was two hundred and seventy-five dollars. Too steep for me. I decided to put in a closed bid.

Hunter's Tip: If you like the element of chance try the closed-bid technique. You simply write your name, address, phone and name of the object on a piece of paper. Put down the price you want to pay. After the sale is over if the piece is still there it may be yours—as the highest or only bidder.

I heard nothing from the seller so I assumed that she had sold the monster for her price. Then, nine months later she called me, and asked if I still wanted the desk. It would be mine for sixty-five dollars, and her two sons would deliver it. The desk is pretty ugly, but it is the answer to a writer's prayer. There are pigeonholes and drawers for everything from bills to typing paper.

The closed bid doesn't always work. But what have you got to lose? Somewhere, sometime I might have found a similar piece for that same price—sixty-five dollars. So far I haven't.

For some reason my best and oldest antiques have cost me little or nothing. And, they are the items people think I am weird to buy. I've become such a jaded hunter that I head automatically for the furniture that is the least likely to have value. A year ago at a basement sale my eyes lit on a painted chest of drawers. Whipping out my trusty tape measure, I checked it at a little over three-feet tall and two-feet three-inches wide. The knobs were wooden and the feet were bracketed. "You can have it for a dollar and a half," said the seller. Oh yes, one other little observation—it was a chest-on-chest and hand-dovetailed. As usual other buyers shook their heads in disbelief. With a little help it was placed in my car and dropped off at the local furniture stripper. I had no idea what was underneath the layers of paint. The woman told me she had bought it at a Salvation Army store fifteen years ago.

Upon its return from the stripper I set about refinishing it with a product called "Wattco." This is a combination of oil and wax and a few secret Danish ingredients. Gradually the wood grain and color emerged as golden maple. Bands of birdseye maple veneer separated the drawers. Was it American or English? The only clue was the inside of the drawers, which were pine. Boning up in the library I learned I had an American country chest-on-chest. Probably it dated before 1850.

One of my beautiful discoveries happened during the closing minutes of a conducted housesale. "Oh, there's nothing left except a nine-hundred-dollar Coromandel screen and a Dresden lamp," I was told.

The sale was in the beautifully furnished apartment of an elderly couple. As I looked at the Coromandel screen I wished for nine hundred dollars and a place to put it. Chunks of quartz, jade, and lapis lazuli jutted out from the black panels. It was a museum piece. I later learned it had been purchased for five hundred dollars by a young couple.

The owner, a man in his seventies, had traveled the world. Wherever he had gone he had sent back gifts to his wife, a collector. Now, she was about to be sent to spend her remaining days in a convalescent home. She sat in her wheelchair in the bedroom as one by one her treasures left through the front door. Her husband told me she wouldn't permit him to sell everything just yet. He planned to move to a one room apartment near the "home."

"As you can see we've sold everything in this room except the screen, lamp, and the chandelier," he said.

He noted that there had been other things in the living room that had been sold as well. He showed me some of his wife's collection of figurines that she was keeping and other objects she had treasured. As I turned to leave I came face-to-face with myself in a mirror, almost hidden behind the living-room door. There was a price tag hanging from it marked twenty-five dollars. But this was no ordinary wall mirror. It appeared to be an eighteenth-century Venetian-glass mirror. Pale green and colorless glass flowers and leaves combined with etched-glass floral designs. Even covered with dust and with missing pieces there was no mistaking it for an antique mirror. But why such a ridiculous price tag placed on it by professional housesale people?

"Everything has to go," was the answer. "Mr. L. wants it out no matter how much it is."

Why had the dealers passed it by? I inquired and learned that this had been a most successful sale, dozens of dealers, hundreds of other browsers and buyers. Yet the mirror remained.

"Maybe nobody bought it because they didn't think it could be repaired," ventured one of the sellers.

"I know it's old," said Mr. L. "I bought it in Venice back in the twenties as an antique." Putting his finger on the etched panel he said, "See, there is no space between my finger and the mirror impression and it's beveled. That's how you tell old glass." He went on to show me the center portion was a replacement and not very old, by the same finger test. This had to be beginner's luck!

Reproductions of this style mirror can be found in decorator shops and very expensive antique galleries for two thousand dollars. Repairs for mine came to fifty-five. Fortunately I found a glass artisan who had a collection of old Venetian glass odds and ends. He did a creditable job matching them up and attaching them with wires.

Hunter's Tip: Look behind doors and near doors for objects overlooked by dealers in a rush.

Another mirror, at the opposite end of the price scale, turned up behind a carriage-house door. It was a cherry and maple country style, with the original glass. Here again, I was the last person at a carriage housesale. Absolutely nothing remained but the mirror. The seller laughingly sold it to me for fifty cents. Now it serves quite nicely with the other country pieces in a son's bedroom.

Usually I never have much luck at the elegant old housesales, professionally run. During the last few years prices have been discouraging for the bargain-minded hunter. In many instances as high as shop prices.

Lately some strange things have been happening. Like bringing in or "planting" new and old objects to pad a sale.

Hunter's Tip: Be suspicious of the sale in posh high-rise apartments or newer homes where there seem to be more furs than one person could wear, or antiques that don't seem to fit in with the general decor of the house. Sales of this type often overprice everything—from antiques to reproductions.

The phony garage sale falls in this category. Pity the poor hunter who thinks he has discovered a spectacular antique-filled garage. The only things bothering him are the high prices and the fact that something isn't quite right. The dangers are two-fold.

1. This is a professionally conducted garage sale. Often the pros aren't very ethical and will go to great lengths to gyp the buyer.

2. Unless you are an expert you'll be so overwhelmed by the sheer number of antiques and collectibles you won't pay attention to the reproductions or downright fakes.

At one of these "pro" garage sales I purchased what I thought was a Currier and Ives print, in a crummy frame, for ten dollars. Foolishly I didn't remove the back to examine the print. For ten dollars, I reasoned, the least I could have would be a reproduction of the print. Besides, wasn't there mold and dirt on the glass and the decaying wood back? I bought quite a few odds and ends and fortunately paid by check. Dashing home I took the back off the picture. Imagine my shock when it turned out to be a torn-off 1957 calendar page.

I am well aware that some people consider these calendar pages highly collectible. They go for two dollars apiece or more at antique shows. I would have settled for a reproduction on heavy paper—but not ten dollars for a calendar page. Back it went and after furious arguments I got my money back.

Another couple I know of have basement sales quite often that are advertised as "must settle estate," or "cleaning out grandma's basement." They buy at the real private housesales and resell to the unwary. This particular duo specializes in stuffing old magazine prints into frames and selling them as authentic prints. They look pretty realistic, till you take off the back.

Hunter's Tip: Take a small screwdriver with you when hunting for artwork. Don't hesitate to use it if you are a serious shopper. No honest seller could object. If they do pass it by.

One of the true tests of a genuine garage sale will be genuine junk from old clothes to leftover ice skates and shower curtains. That's the kind you want.

The only trap for housesale hunters is dating an object

by ownership. Whatever you do, don't buy a piece for a high price because the seller says, "It belonged to my grandmother and I understand it has always been in the family." The problem is that it may have been bought by grandmother just a few years before she "passed away." Also, it may be a fine reproduction that the family has always accepted as being authentic. The problem is that the seller confuses sentiment for value and overprices the object.

At a recent conducted housesale a charming lady's desk in Chippendale style was priced at seventy-five dollars. Because the sale was conducted in a Victorian home, to settle the estate of an elderly woman, most buyers assumed everything in it was quite old. There were in truth many beautiful pieces of circa 1865 furniture, and a couple of obvious late eighteenth-century pieces. So, at first glance, the desk could presumably be authentic—or a fine reproduction, from the early Victorian period. A friend pounced on it, because the sellers proclaimed it very old. And, seventy-five dollars is most reasonable for a desk of any kind these days. Did she bother to look at the dovetailing on the drawers? Did she check the inside for signatures? Was she even suspicious that it was in such good condition? Only when she got it home did she see a label on the back designating it had come from a very fine, and still in business, furniture store. It was a nice twentieth-century reproduction. No, she wasn't gypped. She doesn't care that much whether it is a reproduction. And, it is a bargain for seventy-five dollars.

Odds and ends in porcelain and glass can be the beginning of a fine collection. The hunter with only a dollar to spend can do very well sometimes for a quarter.

Hunter's Tip: A single pressed-glass or cut-glass open saltcellar for a quarter or even a dollar can be a small beginning to an unusual collection of antiques. Buying "singles" of demitasse or cocoa cups will have a collective value. It is easier to pick up a piece here and there—and cheaper. Then, should you sell, it will have value as a collection. You have a good chance simply because the seller won't attach any value to a "broken" set piece.

Hunter's Tip: A mix-match collection of different patterns can be more interesting than the usual matching set.

Show your individuality by serving a dinner party on "singles" antique porcelain. Each piece has a story of its own to tell—and can lend some interesting anecdotes to even the dullest gathering. After all what's wrong with one Haviland or one Wedgwood?

Spoon collectors have been doing mix-match collecting for a long time. Try your luck with handmade napkins, silverware, and serving dishes.

Very often one or two beautiful napkins with hand-done needlework will be on sale for a nickel each. Don't pass them by. Just keep collecting. This mix-match philosophy is ideal for informal buffet serving. After all, anybody can match up. How many people can show enough creativity to mix-match their antiques? Decorators call it "eclectic." You can call it budget.

A single Imari, transfer print, or Majolica plate often turns up in attics and basements for a couple of dollars. Since most sellers and buyers know there is a value to singles in specific patterns and makes, they'll be higher at conducted housesales. Even so, a three-dollar Imari plate is cheaper than a twenty-five-dollar shop-price for an Imari.

If you don't recognize the markings, even with your magnifying glass, but you like it—buy it. Hopefully you haven't paid more than a couple of dollars. If you think it might be Meissen or something equally yummy, dash home to William Chaffers' *Collector's Handbook of Marks and Monograms* and flip through the pages. Be suspicious of complete sets with famous marks. Chances are they are one of the many reproductions made of everything from Meissen to *famille rosé.*

Not too long ago the housesale conductors were trying to "move" a complete set of Oriental-pattern dinnerware. They insisted it was old. It had some Oriental markings on the bottom. Fortunately I had seen a similar set in a local department store. The paper label saying "Made in Japan" apparently had been removed from these pieces. Instead I opted for an old Imari plate for three dollars.

The cut-glass craze is going strong and as you probably know, prices are high. There are two things to be wary of when buying supposedly old cut glass.

1. If it has a cloudy appearance don't buy it. Chances are it is "sick" glass. All the handy-dandy formulas won't give it back a sparkle—regardless of what the seller says.

2. Many pieces of cut glass were marked (acid-etched) with the trademark or maker's name. Today reproductions come from Czechoslovakia, Poland, Germany, and Italy by the boatload. Be careful of buying patterns in feather, pinwheel, fan, and pineapple—popular old patterns. The bases on the new pieces are thick and overall they are heavy. When you are familiar with the old pieces, the new "just don't look the same."

In my first hunting days I was an early bird at a relative's housesale. Many of the Victorian furniture pieces had been earmarked for favored nephews and nieces. For some reason no claim had been staked out on a cut-glass tankard pitcher. Unless you are a serious cut-glass collector, you may not know one pattern from another. Or, even where to look for a signature. There were no clues for me as to age or origin. But, I thought it was outstanding. The relative asked if I thought fifteen dollars too much to pay. What would you have said? After many trips to the library, I found the pattern "Brunswick" and the maker—Thomas Hawkes (one of the founders of Steuben Co.). However, to be authentic it should have a signature. Happily the book told the reader to look under the handle for a Hawkes' mark.

Hunter's Tip: Look on the flat surface of the glass for signs of a trademark. Not only was the pitcher a Thomas Hawkes, but it had won a prize for design at the Columbian Exposition in 1893. Once you have seen quality cut glass you'll have an easy time recognizing other good pieces—whether or not they are marked.

It isn't a good idea to buy a piece of cut glass strictly because you find a mark on it. Some unscrupulous sellers are putting etched decals with Hawkes' signature on some pretty lousy-looking pressed glass. One spotted was a vase for ninety dollars at a shop. The sellers' argument is, of course, "It is a signed Thomas Hawkes." Don't rely on any knowledge but your own, unless you are really sure the seller is a specialist in fine cut glass.

For a while glass baskets could be found everywhere for a couple of dollars. No more. Even the new copies are from eight dollars up. It's up to you to discover them at garage and attic sales. They were popular at the turn of the century in a variety of sizes. The small ones, especially those designed by Frederick Carder (a partner of Thomas Hawkes), are worth looking for.

A collection of cruets, even without stoppers, may be less expensive than old bottles—and just as attractive. Quite accidentally, I found a blown-glass cruet, complete with rough pontil mark, and etched floral design. Even though it had no stopper and two tiny chips on the neck, I bought it—for a dollar. It looked quite lonely in a cupboard with new Quimper and Depression glass. In fact, the cruet was one of the last remnants of a two-day housesale. Even as I stood there the Quimper and Depression glass were swept from the shelves.

Keep in mind at all times that this is "the age of kitsch." Just because everybody else thinks anything is collectible from Kewpie dolls to old shoe lasts, don't believe it. Keep a cool head. Resist the urge to buy everything in sight at a housesale. If you are a beginning collector-hunter, test your willpower. Visit several housesales and *don't buy a thing*—unless it is very, very unusual. Otherwise your house will look like somebody's housesale.

One woman who conducts housesales professionally admits she was an early victim of her own sales. Now she has a collection of demitasse cups, cut glass, etc. The entire house is a mass of collections. At least she admits it. Another collector-dealer is less fortunate. Even though I've never been inside her home, it sounds frightening. She collects Oriental rugs, snuff bottles, and on and on. Apparently she can't stop collecting just one more thing—or starting just one more new collection. The ultimate shock comes when you try to get rid of your "overbuys" and nobody else is collecting them. That is why you often see the same people holding house and garage sales month after month. They are amateur collectors trying to get rid of their overbuys. By now every hunter is wise and has been to their sales a couple of times. The only thing they can do is put it all in boxes and let it "age" for five years. If they are lucky, by then the world will have forgotten the address—and they can have a successful sale.

A Louis XVI *secretaire à abattant* (fall-front desk) that you could have bought for one hundred fifty dollars at my first housesale—many years ago. If you had visited enough museums you would have recognized it for what it was. Close examination would show you the obvious signs of age—genuine wormholes in the interior drawers; slight warping of the top and the doors. Inside, the pigeonhole compartment comes out to reveal a secret (fake) compartment. The dovetails on the top drawer consist of one very large piece and two smaller ones at each end. Typical work of the eighteenth century. It is five feet high. The back wood is very rough, since the piece was made to be set against the wall. To add to the mystery of its maker, part of a signature in chalk was visible on the back—but couldn't be made out. Should it turn out the marquetry was done by a master of the art, such as Charles Topino or Jean François Oeban, its value would go up . . . since Oeban didn't sign his pieces, and did specialize in secret drawers. Who knows?

Another clue to the age of the *secretaire*—the original key. Made of brass, it is somewhat crude and obviously handwrought.

A close-up of the fall front shows the detail of the neo-classic design. Each piece meticulously cut and matched in a variety of woods.

Early Victorian buffet or sideboard. The end doors swing out. The upper-middle drawer is lined in velvet for silver. At first glance it appears to be Renaissance Revival (1850). Even so, it has hardware made prior to 1830 and hand-dovetailed drawers. But for fate, it would be demolished or still in the basement when I first saw it holding everybody's laundry.

Odds and ends can add up to some
unusual antiques. This pressed-glass
lamp shade was found in a dirty cardboard box in a basement, for a quarter. Turned upside down it is an inexpensive shade for a wall bracket
lamp. It has been reproduced and
sells for several dollars brand new. If
you keep looking you can still find
single glass shades that once covered
old gas-light fixtures. They come in
a variety of patterns. If you are
lucky you may find a cranberry or
hobnail single shade.

Two nineteenth-century mirrors that
were discovered hanging behind doors
at housesales. Both were bypassed till
nearly the end of the sale. The Venetian mirror dates from either the eighteenth or nineteenth century. Pale
green and clear leaves and flowers are
handblown in the fashion of the famous Murano glass. White flowers are
also etched on sections. The entire
mirror is held together with wires.
Contemporary copies will sell for six
hundred dollars. The originals, like this
one, wear price tags of over one
thousand dollars. This was priced at
twenty-five dollars when I spotted it.
A specialist in this type of glass repair
put it back together for fifty-five
dollars. Many dealers didn't want to be
bothered by repairs, didn't know of a
potential buyer, or didn't recognize it
for what it is. The country mirror is
beautiful in its own way, and fits into
a boy's bedroom decorated with American country pieces. It combines walnut with walnut burl trim. For fifty
cents it was quite a find—behind the
door in the garage. The going price
is from thirty-five to forty dollars. It
didn't even need resilvering. I don't
think the dealers even saw it. They
were too busy galloping through grabbing up the items in plain sight.

47

Sometimes housesales come up with real treasures. With one exception, all of these late nineteenth-century bottles came from one housesale. Again, it was almost closing time when I arrived. They were on the fireplace mantle, priced at six dollars each. Two smaller ones were three dollars. The housesale conductor said the reason they were still there was because the dealers had decided they weren't old. Taking a close look, you would see the mold seams go up to the bottle lip —not through it. The exception, is the "Winter-summer" tree bottle. It has a rough pontil, no applied lip, and was made earlier. It was found at a small apartment sale for twenty dollars and is worth much more.

It's not everyday you can buy a signed, Thomas Hawkes pitcher for fifteen dollars. This tankard in the Brunswick pattern won a prize for good design at the 1893 Columbian Exposition. The signature, under the handle, is very hard to see without a magnifying glass. Watch for faked signatures on poor quality pressed glass. If you aren't sure whether a piece is pressed or cut, tap it gently with your finger. It should ring. Also, run your fingers over the pattern. It should feel sharp if it is cut glass.

Back-porch sales yield suprises. Especially popular are old oversized fur coats from the thirties and forties. The mangy muskrat was a discovery for this gal at eight dollars. The antique quilts behind her were offered at twenty-five dollars—but strangely, no takers. It was a day for funky finery hunters.

Country Chippendale or American Country chest-on-chest. Call it whatever you wish, it emerged from layers of paint as walnut, with veneered molding of birdseye maple. Total cost, including stripping and refinishing, came to fifteen dollars. This must have been meant for a child's room because it is only three-and-a-half feet high and a foot deep. It is hard to say whether it was made late eighteenth century, just because of the dovetailing and bracket feet. The inside of the drawers are pine. If they were oak it would be an English piece. Because it took years for furniture fashions to catch on in their move from England to America, the piece could have actually been made anytime up to 1830. The wooden pulls are mushroom shape, which also helps date the piece within that time span. It is comforting to note similar pieces going for over three hundred dollars in the shops.

This Confederate one-hundred-dollar bill was literally washed out of a pine apothecary chest. While there are always a lot of "ifs" when dating an antique, this might come close to dating the chest. The bill isn't worth anything to a collector because of its bad condition. To a story teller it's priceless. It might also be an indication that the chest came originally from Louisiana.

Not everybody appreciates or recognizes a valentine from the 1830s. This hand-colored one was found in a scrapbook at a housesale. At four dollars and fifty cents it was a bargain.

A collection of cruets often begins at an odds-and-ends box in housesales. The owner of this collection spent from a quarter to a dollar for the cruets. Those with a ground-glass stopper are harder to come by. Try picking up a stopper here and there for nickles and dimes. Chances are they will match the cruets. Many cruets were made in the Victorian era by art-glass manufacturers. They are so popular there is a special book published listing many types. As a result they are becoming more difficult to find at hunter's prices.

4

The Spring Rummage Rite

Don't laugh at those funny-looking people you see pouring out of churches most any Thursday in April or May. Note carefully that many of those clutching huge brown shopping bags are wearing fat smiles. They are participating in an important antique hunters' rite—rummaging. If you have a spirit of adventure, you'll soon become one of them.

Every spring the church ladies' sewing circles put on rummage sales. The objects so generously contributed are for the most part garbage-can rejects. Their former owners are convinced that they have no value whatsoever. They are earmarked for church rummage. The most common throw-aways are clothing and kitchen-ware. Table linens and towels run a close third.

Realize too that the church ladies and rummage volunteers always have first choice. Veteran pickers that they are, nothing that even looks remotely like an antique gets past their beady eyes. Any cut-glass bowls, hand-painted china and crystal are snapped up before they ever see the rummage counter.

It would seem at first glance that the chances of finding anything collectible are nil. To the contrary, there are often fantastic finds. The secret of success at rummage is merely to re-orient your concept of what is worth collecting.

To your advantage is the generation gap. Especially if you like freaky antiques. You may not "dig" cut glass, and dainty figurines, so dear to another era. Concentrate on freaky and funky goodies. Old Coca-Cola glasses, typewriters, and metal shoe-lifts are not usually snapped up at rummage. Turn-of-the-century beaded handbags are currently showing up at many a rummage. In good condition they are worth more than the dollar or two you'll pay. To make you feel really good: contemporary French copies are going in boutiques for over forty-five dollars.

Head for the jewelry counter. It always abounds with junky gems from the twenties and thirties. Who cares that the ruby brooches have been grabbed by dealers. What you want are bracelets of celluloid and gaudy rhinestone clasps and buckles, straight out of a Jean Harlow movie.

One important source for rummage is "estates" and worldly goods left to the church by deceased members. What is left after the money is extracted is usually household effects. Picture if you can rooms of fabulous Victorian pieces being left in the overworked hands of a distraught rummage chairman. She couldn't care less about "that old stuff." Better yet, take out a Kleenex while I tell you a sad tale of woe about just such an estate.

I was recently asked to advise the chairman of a church rummage on how to dispose of a deceased member's estate. Proceeds would go to the church. I was assured in advance by the lady, "that really there wasn't much left worth looking at in the five-room apartment." Good-hearted soul that I am, I agreed to help. Besides, there was the possibility of antique hunting in a virgin preserve.

We met first at her home, because she had "brought a few of the things to sort out for rummage"—like a truckload.

Happiness was mine as I plowed through grocery bags filled with old jewelry, books, and kitchenware. There were boxes filled with tiny charms, premiums from early twentieth-century candy boxes. "Oh," said she, "I'm going to throw that cheap stuff out." I stayed her hand from tossing away a mini-locomotive.

Another box contained dozens of Victorian stickpins, tie bars, and cuff links. Apparently the deceased never threw anything out.

"Look at these funny old boxes," said the chairman. The funny boxes were actually handsome, polished, inlaid-wood seed-boxes. They were well over one hundred years old. Their inside covers contained advertisements, colorfully illustrated with flowers and people. "Did you ever see so much junk?" she laughed. "Lordy! You should see what my rummage ladies threw out over at the apartment."

I winced. The mere thought of what treasures lurked in that apartment garbage can—at that very moment—nearly sent me into shock. I tried to keep my hunter's composure. "All of these things have a value—to a collector," I said. "Please don't throw anything at all out." I suggested we leave instantly for the apartment. On the way she said she would appreciate my advice on how best to dispose of the apartment remains—and what the "junk could be sold for." Supposedly the ladies' committee had removed the best things for rummage. She planned to go over the things I had just viewed and pitch most into the garbage can. "The old scrapbooks with the advertising trade cards and valentines."

"There's really not much to see," she apologized. "We gave a twelve-piece set of crystal and some glass to the minister's wife. And, of course, the ladies took most of the cut glass and china."

The more we talked the stronger grew the scent of antique treasures. It seemed the late owner had never married and had no close relatives, when she expired at age ninety.

"You've never seen such a place," said the chairman, pulling up to the curb. "Those old lamps with the glass shades were all over the place. But I got rid of those right away. The landlady and her daughter liked them. Wait until you see the buffet. It's a real monstrosity with all that carving."

The apartment was a two-flat in an old city neighborhood. We got the key from the elderly Polish landlady. She followed us, telling me her life history and asking if any of the things were worth anything. "I liked those old lamps. My daughter put them down in the basement to give some light over the laundry tubs." I thought I was going to faint—Tiffany and washtubs.

My hunter's scent had been correct. The apartment was a dream. A round oak dining table faced a huge, early Victorian buffet. Both were littered with collectibles of every description. "Look at these old marbles," said the chairman. "Aren't they funny-looking with these animals inside?" She was holding a large plate filled with sulphide marbles, circa 1900. Their value: up to fifty dollars each.

"Promise me," I begged, practically groveling, "you won't throw anything out until I can come back and look again?" She thought I was bananas, but gave me her word.

Scattered about were several beaded handbags, hand-painted unmatched demitasse cups and old pieces of pressed glass.

In one bedroom reposed a circa 1836 iron-and-brass bed, dainty scrolled like a valentine. An Empire chest and an Eastlake desk stood nearby. The other bedroom contained a towering mahogany headboard-bed and chest.

Even the kitchen was a treasure trove. A huge oak worktable with spool legs shared space with a small Victorian washstand. Near the door were brown bags and boxes destined for the garbage. "That's what the ladies tossed out," she said.

I rescued two tin 1933 World's Fair banks, a tortoiseshell comb and some handmade embroidered towels. There were old thimbles, button boxes . . . literally enough to open a shop with.

Now for the moment of truth. I couldn't buy everything. But, I resolved to spend a few minutes and at least tell the lady some estimated values. I suggested a reliable conducted-housesale group to come in and sell everything down to the bare bones. As I explained, the seller would take twenty percent. All the bothersome price tagging, etc. would be out of her hair. Plus, that way I could come to the sale and select one or two items at a reasonable price. I had visions of the church making a couple of thousand dollars.

When a week passed and I had no word from either the housesale group or the chairman, I called. "Oh," she said. "I decided to call in a dealer. Would you believe he took all that stuff off my hands for two hundred dollars. And, I decided to hold on to some of the pieces you seemed to think were so valuable. We'll use it in a special antique show at church."

Meanwhile, the "junk" is in the chairman's attic. I hope she stays in good health till the antique sale. Otherwise it's another coup for the junkman.

Now, for a few realistic facts about attending an actual church rummage. Get there early, go in fighting, and don't pull any punches. Carry your big brown shopping bag. You have to work fast. The pros get there early. In a flash they grab items and stuff them into their bags. No time to leisurely deliberate. If you take time for a second glance—the object is gone. Besides, how far wrong can you go for a nickel or dime?

At every rummage there is a designated "treasure room." This is where you'll find stray pieces of Flow Blue, cut glass, and whatever the ladies' committee didn't want. Not everything in the treasure room is an antique or a treasure. There is always plenty of made-yesterday statuary, ash trays, and silver salt-and-pepper sets. This is where the dealers strike first, shoveling like mad into their bags.

That is one reason why you should go to either the picture frame–art counter or the kitchenware–miscellaneous first. You'd be surprised how many small gilt Victorian frames and authentic old art prints show up for nickels and dimes. In kitchenware the possibilities are endless. Look for the colorful spatter enamelware from the early 1900s. This comes in bright blues, greens, and yellows. At this particular sale, I found a Turk's mold and a pie pan in blue for ten cents each. The mold is now a novel planter in my kitchen. The pie pan hangs on the wall.

Guess what ended up on the miscellaneous counter? Why, that groovy little World's Fair bank—for a quarter. I also recognized other objects I had rescued from the garbage can. A fanciful old rug beater and several pieces of woodenware were saved for an appreciative collector.

Rack upon rack of funky clothes were being snapped up by the under-thirty crowd. The elderly volunteers watched it all with incredulous eyes.

Rummage is big business for one wealthy suburban Chicago congregation. For the last two years their gross has been between forty and sixty thousand for one eight-hour day. In fact, this one is so big, it takes up an entire block and three floors of the church community building. Free buses shuttle from train and bus directly to the church. Six hundred and forty volunteers sort, price and sell. The line begins forming at 3:00 A.M. for the 7:00 A.M. opening. Contributions of rummage come from Wisconsin, Indiana, and Illinois. As usual, workers get first choice—the day before the sale. The only thing to console you is that not everybody is looking for antiques. Or, for the type of antique you may be looking for. Also, the late arrival gets items for half price. Hopefully, there are a few things left after 4:00 P.M.

If you thing this rummage is particularly good, you can depend on it that other hunters think so too. They bring thermoses of coffee and prepare to stand in line for a couple of pre-opening hours.

At the "big one" I arrived late. An old country-style dining chair, circa 1890, was left for fifty cents . . . and an Empire sideboard for a hundred dollars. The problem with a big piece, even at a bargain price, is cartage. Unless you have a truck or trailer of your own and a strong friend, add twenty dollars or more to your purchase price. But, how or where else can you find an authentic Empire sideboard for under two hundred dollars? Possibly at a house or garage sale. But, do you have the faith and patience to pass this one up in the hopes of finding another?

In a case such as this, bargain with the rummage ladies. They don't plan to carry the big pieces home either. You'll never know if you don't try. Forget your pride. Offer fifty dollars and see what happens.

When it's all over where do the leftovers go? Sometimes to charitable institutions. More likely the Salvation Army truck carries it all away.

If you don't score at one, remember there's always another rummage sale going on—somewhere—in the spring.

Brown-bag treasures from a couple of church rummage sales. The best finds of the lot are the small lacy sandwich-type footed dish, for fifty cents and primitive hand-carved man's head (in seed box) cost a quarter.

A 1933 Chicago World's Fair give-away, is this tin-can bank. It was saved from the garbage—and wound up at a rummage for a dollar. Originally it was made by the American Can Company, in several designs. This one shows the famous "sky ride" and Art Deco architecture.

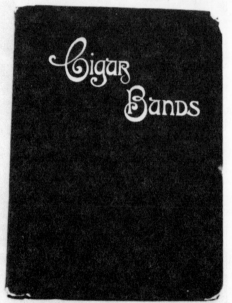

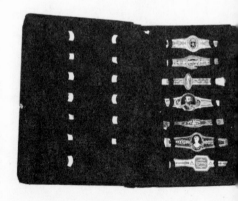

Remember wearing those cigar bands on your finger when you were a kid? Now they're highly desirable to freaky collectors. There are even a couple of collections in permanent exhibit at quality museums. These were in good condition and mounted in their own album—ready for rummage.

Beaded bags like these leftovers from Victorian days go for four dollars at rummage—if you are lucky. The inside may be lined with chamois or silk. The one on the left says "Made in France." The new ones from France are quite a bit more expensive. Even at conducted housesales oldies are priced at from twenty-five to forty-five dollars. Many collectors frame them and mount them on the wall.

Seedbox made from polished cedar. Both lock and hinges are delicately designed in brass. Another rummage refugee. The advertising message is still bright and fresh looking, protected on the inside of the lid.

An early pressed-glass cup, possibly a child's (left), and a turn-of-the-century etched-glass mustard pot. Fifty cents apiece on the rummage tray. The cup is now being reproduced and selling for six dollars. The mustard pot has a silver top.

Indian dolls were once inexpensive and plentiful and everyone seemed to bring one back from their vacations in the 1930s. Today they may show up at rummage sales at bargain prices. Keep your eyes open if they are your "thing."

Satsuma and hand-painted porcelain at rummage? Well, at any rate these miniatures were found on a rummage table. They are doll-house size.

Crackerjack charms from the turn-of-the-century may look like junk jewelry to nonaficionados. They're good as gold to the freaky hunter who buys them for pennies at rummage sales.

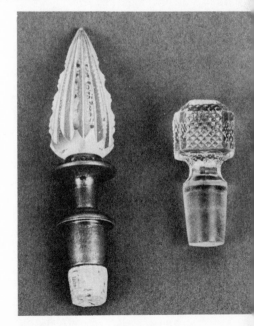

Don't pass by stoppers without bottles. They can be a collection in themselves. Since many people consider them worthless, even the cut-glass beauty (left) can end up in the basement junk box. Keep your eye out for interesting shapes in both cut glass or pressed. The pressed stopper (right) is beginning to turn purple.

Flower seedbox makes a perfect gift for organic-food fanciers or a jewelry box for a teenager. This was saved from church rummage. Best place is at country auctions or estate sales at farmhouses. The large bulk-size seedboxes are harder to find.

I hoped at first glance this was a signed Gibson Girl drawing. No such luck. It's still a good rummage buy for a quarter.

This rare H. Bunbury print was a rummage find for one dollar. If you want to save even more money, offer to buy the print without the frame for less. Chances are you will want to re-mat and frame anyhow. Bunbury was a famous British artist-satirist. Found at the same rummage, a French aquatint, Pollard coaching print, and a J. M. W. Turner engraving—all for a dollar each. This particular rummage is held in a very wealthy area and buyers come from miles around to flip through the rummage.

5

The Antique Snob—
Should You Trap One
When You Find One?

THE ANTIQUE SNOB is not becoming extinct. In fact, he or she is just changing methods of disguise. Any antique hunter with experience has come to recognize the telltale signs of the bona fide antique snob. Regardless of whether they fall into the category of fancier or freak, they can be trapped—if you want to bother. Sometimes it's more fun to be smug and silent.

In the early days of antique hunting, the snob generally was affluent. Money was no object as his hired buyer tracked the four corners of the world bringing back succulent antique morsels. They often bypassed collecting for gluttony, gobbling up anything that even hinted of Louis Quatorze or Chippendale. They assumed it was the real thing because they had paid a fortune for it. Alas, after their demise, their heirs learned otherwise. Many of the so-called authenticated pieces turned up at auction and were discovered to be—reproductions.

Hunter's Tip: Money doesn't necessarily buy happiness —or authentic antiques.

While shopping in a resale shop funded by a group of society matrons, I ran into a very collectible type of antique snob. They can be recognized by their possessiveness. They begin every sentence with "my." One lady in the shop referred to "My Dr. Wall." And "My Louis Quatorze." If you didn't know better, you would think she was on a first-name basis with the good doctor and someone named Louis. It is a great opportunity to ask "Louis who?" In fact, my companion nudged me and asked who Dr. Wall was. Once outside, I explained that Dr. John Wall manufactured Worcester porcelain from 1751 to his death in 1776. Dr. Wall was an excellent artist and etched several plates and designed stained-glass windows. Needless to say, porcelain of this period is quite scarce and expensive. So, if you are on a speaking basis with Dr. Wall, that intimates you are a collector of great wealth and status.

The second clue found at the resale shop was the use of the words "Louis Quatorze." As an instructor in the local antiques class advised the beginners, "Always refer to Louis XIV as Louis Quatorze. This automatically establishes you as being knowledgeable."

Another clue is pronouncing words like Steuben and Parke-Bernet and Winterthur. In some instances, the snow is correct—in others pronunciation can be as you wish it. Like tomato and to-MAH-to. It is Steuben or

SteuBEN? Parke-Bernet or Parke-BerNAY? Winter-thur or WinterTER? Does anyone really care? Oh yes, the antique snob does.

Snobbishness by association is another distinguishing characteristic. It's like being on a first-name basis with your decorator. You casually mention William Pahlman as "Will" or "Will Baby" depending on whether or not you are over thirty. Knowing the owner of the most posh auction house or most expensive antique gallery by first name is de rigueur. "Let me call my man at the Gilded Coach Gallery—you know, Wilfred?" If you don't know Wilfred, you just put yourself in peasant category. Note also: the owner of an antique shop is the owner of an antique gallery.

Visiting the antique snob's home is a dead giveaway. There is usually an impressive library or book-wall of leather-bound classics. This is what decorators refer to as *buying books by-the-yard.* Madame wanted antique books to match the new-old Oriental rugs. The decorator had to purchase enough leather-bound books to cover space twenty feet by nine feet. And, the colors must be right. Usually favored are the signed, numbered complete sets of the author's works. They were popular in the early 1900s, and are similar to book-of-the-month-club selections. Many are beautiful to flip through, boasting colored engravings. But, like I said, they are bought by-the-yard, not the book. You can often find a handsome set at a housesale. I now own the complete works of Honoré de Balzac, with color engravings, for ten dollars. Housesale, circa 1970.

You'll also note a preponderance of Queen Anne and Chippendale pieces. Especially popular are Queen Anne lowboys. Nothing but Georgian silver will do—and of course, Dr. Wall or Oriental Lowestoft.

If you are a sneaky hunter, and you really want to

trap the snob, check out the authenticity of those chairs and the lowboy. At the next big party whip out your magnifying glass and magnet. While the others are sipping drinks, crawl under the Queen Anne bureau-bookcase to see if it says made by Jones's Department Store. Casually start opening drawers to look for labels, and dovetailing details. It's no worse than the snob who turns over your demitasse to check whether it's a name-dropping name. All's fair in love, war, and antique hunting.

The antique snobs can be recognized by attitude. They will let you know upon first meeting that they know absolutely everything there is to know about fine antiques. Or, freaky collectibles. Remember, the snob isn't just a fancier. There are Depression-glass and Avon-bottle snobs as well. If anything, the freaky snobs seem to be more numerous—and easier to trap these days. Instead of wanting a few choice postcards or vintage radios, they have not only an entire room of empty beer cans but a can or two scattered about their contemporary two-hundred-thousand-dollar pad. The freaky-collector snob tends to be very greedy. If one or two advertising tins are good, two hundred are better.

The freaky snob tends to take himself and his collection very seriously. I shall long remember the time I mislabeled a gasoline iron in one of my newspaper columns. Would you believe I had dozens of letters from irate collectors of old irons demanding public retractions; apologies for not being more serious about such an important area of collecting! One writer had a collection of over two hundred irons of all descriptions. Well, you never know when they could come in handy. It is just very difficult to take a collection of ten thousand empty beer cans seriously.

Gradually increasing are the American-primitive

snobs. Money is no object for an old jelly cupboard or linen chest. Do they go to country auctions and little shops in farm communities? Heavens no. They find an expensive gallery that specializes in American primitives. While many of their purchases may be authentic handcrafted pine and maple, many won't be. There is a very thriving business these days in made-to-order American primitives at high prices. They are beautiful to look at, and generally in near-perfect condition. Unfortunately, the American-primitive snob assumes they are authentic because the price was hefty. He or she is basically no different than the Dr. Wall or freaky snob, in one respect. They know absolutely everything. Except they forgot to check out the width of the boards on the back of the cherry corner-cabinet and to look for signs of weathering or aging color. It's best not to tangle with them over authenticity. They are ready to do battle at the drop of a squareheaded nail. Let them live in their forest of fantasy until they decide to "sell off a few pieces." As you by now realize, to them the place where an object is purchased and the high price are more important than authenticity. Keep combing those basements and garages. When you try to sell off some of your American-primitive finds you may be money ahead of the snob collector.

One of my collecting acquaintances came back from a London trip bright-eyed and full of tales of wonder about London shops and dealers. "They're so different from American antique dealers. Why, they're charming. And, their antiques are really old. They don't seem to be at all interested in Oriental things. That would be a good place to shop for Chinese pieces, don't you think?"

My friend is well on her way to becoming an antique snob. "London" is always a good name to drop. Soon she will acquire the names of a couple of expensive shops and become possessive of "my little dealer in London."

I mentioned offhandedly that there were more Queen Anne chairs in London now than there were in Queen Anne's day. I considered mentioning what a serious collector had told me about a recent trip to London. "It's nothing new. Most of the London dealers come over to the United States for their antiques—especially to the Midwest."

So, the American collector may wind up paying for the dealer's travel expenses, plus shipping back to the United States. Hopefully, after all of that, the piece is authentic. No wonder London dealers are so charming to American browsers. It is wise to remember the famous Shrager court case in 1923. A wealthy collector had purchased what he had hoped were antique oak-paneled walls from a historic residence, "Royston Hall." As it turned out, despite many dealers testifying the paneling was Elizabethan, it had been made to order for the victim. There was no such place as Royston Hall, only a Royston dairy. A couple of scraps of paneling were taken from the dairy and used as a "model" for the reconstructed room. It took an old, experienced carpenter to point out to the "experts" that the walls had been made with modern tools. How many ads have you read lately concerning historical paneled walls "taken from an old abbey" or "removed from an old castle"? What antique snob could resist such a lure? If you would decorate with old English or what-have-you paneling, take a tip from Mr. Shrager and take your friendly carpenter with you to examine the work. It's cheaper to pay his fare to England or France than to pay thousands for worthless decor. It took many experts long hours to discover that these walls had been skillfully "faked." Is there any reason to believe that authentic English oak antique paneling can't be purchased by-the-yard—and is made to order?

"Oh, you're hung up on reproductions," one of my antique expert friends sneered. Possibly. But perhaps it's because I'm not an expert that I'm wary.

Antique Snob Glossary

Here are a few words to start you on your way to being a successful antique or "collectible" snob. Doubtless you'll add a few of your own as you become more of an "expert." Just remember that when you "drop" these names, you must have an air of total authority. This will eliminate any doubt and save you from embarrassing questions by another "expert." It will send him or her back to re-examine their collections. And possibly switch from Dr. Wall to Meissen.

There are no definitions included on the list for one very simple reason. If you don't know what the object is that you are name dropping—you have no business trying to become a bona fide antique snob.

For the serious snob, I have included names that are no longer being dropped. Or, if they are, they no longer mean anything. Just as fashions change, so do fashions in antiques and collectibles. The market value proves this point. When objects begin to slip at auction they have momentarily, at least, had their day with the antique snob. After all, who would want to drop a name only to learn that it went at auction for a fraction of what the snob had paid several years ago. Being eternally on top of what's happening is a must for the practicing snob. To lose track is to lose face. Realize that the following glossary may be completely obsolete by the time you read this. In that case use it in the past tense as follows: "When I used to collect my little Bow figures—" or "I gave my collection of ivories to the thrift shop for their flea market." Meantime, of course, you merely pack the objects away till you see signs of interest at auction.

GLOSSARY

In	Out
Dr. Wall (especially Worcester wares)	Dorothy Doughty birds
	Carnival glass
Art Deco. The ultimate would be a 1933 Chicago World's Fair poster, or a piece by Rene Lalique	Limited editions of practically anything
	R. S. Prussia
	Beam bottles
Oriental Lowestoft (especially Fitzhugh with American eagle motif)	Jade figurines
	Stradivari violins
	Endangered species
Old Hawaiian bottles	Trophies
Tachi-do (Japanese armour)	Queen Anne lowboys
Edison phonograph	Pre-Columbian anything
Shrunken heads	Coca-Cola collectibles
American primitive furniture	Roll-top desk
American Indian anything	Antiquities from other countries
Advertising mirrors, tins	Georgian silver candelabra
Schoolmaster's desk	
Architectural fragments from demolished American buildings	
A silver askos	

An askos has to be the ultimate snob object—mainly because few people know what one is, or even what it is used for. Give Thomas Jefferson the credit for introducing the askos to America. The originals were of clay and bronze, discovered by archeologists excavating at Herculaneum and Pompeii in the late eighteenth century. Jefferson saw an askos while visiting in France. He commissioned a silversmith to create one for him. He was well aware that an askos is a *urinal*. Apparently he had a great sense of humor since it was used on his dining table filled with syrup or honey.

Meanwhile, a couple of hundred years have passed and suddenly some silver askos are beginning to appear with the name Paul Storr imprinted, and the dates 1834 and 1836. They are being sold as *wine jugs* for hundreds of dollars to—who but the antique snob? Little does he or she know that the word *askos* means "bag" or "bladder."

The antique snob is safe. After all who would dare ask what that silver boot on the table is?

These rediscovered silver ewers have miraculously been appearing on the market since an article appeared in the July, 1973 *Antiques* magazine. By December 1973 a similar "pair" of askos were offered for sale as wine jugs by expensive shops in London and the U.S.

The following is probably the most important information any antique snob can be privy to.

I could never understand why everyone referred to Sotheby Parke-Bernet as "Parke-BerNAY." I didn't even feel secure about the pronunciation when the auction house answered "Sotheby Parke-BerNET" on the telephone. Could my fanciest friends and purist collectors who dropped the august name continually be wrong about such an important matter?

Bravely I phoned a Mr. Clark Nelson, chargé d'affaires for the auction gallery.

"It is Sotheby Parke-BerNET," he said. "After all, Otto Bernet was a Swiss-German. Hiram Parke was English." I rest my case.

How many people do you know who own a genuine, circa 1820, French sedan chair? This was purchased at auction for a mere fifteen hundred dollars by a dealer. It is equipped with a French phone and light. This has to be the ultimate in antique gamesmanship—for a price.

—*Courtesy*: Chicago Art Gallery

Sometimes money is no object for a status collectible. This gilded throne chair with red velvet seat is a must for the nostalgia buff. It once graced the lobby of a Balaban and Katz movie theater. A dedicated hunter tracked it down at auction for seven hundred and fifty dollars.

—*Courtesy*: Chicago Art Gallery

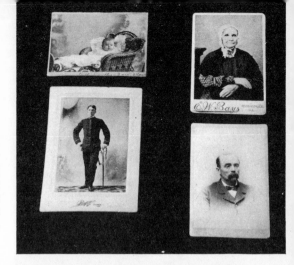

A built-in family tree for the antique snob—old photos. For a few cents, you too can find distinguished appearing ancestors or prove your "roots" go back a long time. This is cheaper than buying a primitive oil portrait or large tintype portraits.

The Swee-Touch-Nee Tea tin is a very big seller at Advertising tin shows. The original, that is. This one can still be purchased filled with tea for a dollar and a quarter or so at your supermarket. Hopefully, the freaky snob knows the difference between the old and new.

Perhaps it's really just nostalgia that makes souvenirs from the great ocean liners so popular. However, you must admit it is the ultimate in snobbery to have a complete set of silver, porcelain, or one of these signed crystal goblets from the captain's table on the *Ile de France*. One man has made a fortune with ships' salvage from the ocean liners. This is St. Louis cut crystal. At one such salvage, tacky deck chair blankets with the ship's name embroidered on them were selling like crazy for ten dollars and up. Yes, it does lend the ultimate touch draped over a Mies Van Der Rohe Barcelona chair.

Everybody knows a Tiffany when they see one. For nineteen thousand five hundred dollars, this one added some status in the right place. If you don't have something Tiffany, where are you these days?
—*Courtesy*: Chicago Art Gallery

The Queen Anne desk, circa early 1700s, is a must for the antique snob. Luckily for him it has been reproduced often. This one is authentic and was found by a serious collector with twelve thousand dollars to invest.

The delight of the freaky antique snob is one or more pinball machines or slot machines. The earlier, the better—and the more expensive. Because so many slot machines have been destroyed over the years and considered "illegal," the price for those still around continues to go up. Your local nostalgia shop may put you on the waiting list—provided you are willing to come up with several hundred dollars at the proper time. The ultimate would be an 1895 slot machine complete with spades, hearts, bells, diamonds, horseshoes, and stars. Alas, no jackpot. Find a slot machine made after 1907 and you've literally hit the jackpot. Mechanical games of skill are equally "in" with the antique snob, especially racing vintage autos at a miniature Grand Prix.

The nostalgia snob will think nothing of paying a bundle of cash for an old perfume-vending machine. Just for kicks he can keep it filled with the most expensive fragrance on the market. What could be more "in" than for him to invite his female guests to "help yourself to some of that new Courreges, 'Empreinte.'"

Pre-Columbian figurines were very "in" with status collectors for many a year. This Ecuador Esmeraldas is a fertility idol in terra-cotta—3 x 6 inches. You might find a similar one at auction—or private collection—for twenty to fifty dollars.

—*Courtesy*: Harmer Rooke
Numismatists Ltd.

You must admit there is something different about this chain and the baskets carved from discarded peach pits and wood. No, you don't wear them. You frame them with a plaque that reads, "Authentic American primitive carving, circa 1860." Be sure to have the name of an expensive gallery on a tiny corner label. While it's more fun if your own grandfather carved them while he was waiting for the Civil War to end, there isn't as much status.

Brace yourself! You are looking at an authentic American primitive whats-it. Take it from Sotheby Parke-Bernet —American primitives like this one are the coming antique collectibles. Antique snobs will be trying to outbid each other for these new-old status symbols. Get the jump on all of them. Go to more attic and garage sales. Maybe you'll be lucky and find one like this for fifty cents. Note the genuine splint seat and the "score" marks on the legs. Can it be Shaker —and worth much more than fifty cents?

6

Hunting From Auction House to Pawnshop— and Blindfolded

BREATHES THERE A hunter who has never tried his luck at an auction? Since early Roman days auctions have been a favorite sport. Today, there are dozens of kinds offering everything from antiques to bicycles. There are auctions held in fancy galleries, store fronts, homes, docks, restaurants, warehouses, towns and farms, post offices and commercial buildings. Take your choice— and your money. Good or bad, they are at worst interesting; at best, the peak of excitement. At auctions you can see what you are bidding on.

For the hunter who likes the element of chance there

is the Russian Roulette auction or container sale. You don't see what is inside the container; maybe you win, maybe you lose. You pay from one hundred and fifty dollars up for the privilege of taking this chance.

Time was when attending auctions was something akin to opening night at the opera: you dressed. There was a certain status in letting it be known you were on your way to Sotheby Parke-Bernet or the Chicago Art Gallery or their equivalents. Today, everybody is auction-conscious. And why not when there are auctions every day of the week—practically anywhere you live.

There is something for everybody. At the top of the list are still the old names that draw bidders like Jackie O. and various movie personalities. The hunt here is for nearly priceless art objects. Ten thousand dollars for a single paperweight or fourteen thousand for a Chippendale desk are a mere whimsy for bidders at the gilt-edged auctions. Unless you have a few million stashed away, it's best to restrain yourself at this type of auction. However, once in a while you may find something at your price.

Auction Hunter's Tip: Generally you should check the mailing pieces or ads to see what the featured items are—from Oriental rugs to Chinese bronzes. Next, check out box-lots or miscellaneous items. Then you use your common sense and realize the rugs and bronzes will be drawing the majority of bidders. The single miscellaneous item or box-lot will be your opportunity for a bid— and a bargain.

Breaking it down still further, see if there are any single items of interest that are difficult to come by at reasonable prices—like a Shaker piece at a city auction. If something does interest you get there early enough to find a seat within good eye view of the auctioneer.

Anne Gilbert

Previewing Is a Must

You may not even want that Shaker chair or other objects when you see them close up. Perhaps they don't look authentic. Or, perhaps you discover the piece is better than you hoped—a rarity that isn't accurately described. For instance, a Shaker piece might be designated as "country style" or "Shaker style." If so, and your scrutiny proves otherwise you may be a winner at the auction. Take the head of the auction house aside and inquire as to what he thinks the object may go for. If the answer is in your price range, plan to be there and bid. It may go for more—or hopefully to you, for less. It's a truism that many bidders are bidding for a moneyed buyer, who wishes to remain incognito—or simply doesn't want to be bothered attending. These bidders have advance instructions as to what to bid on, and within a certain price range. They will come from all over the world if there is something that they know will interest their buyer. They won't be there to bid on that single Shaker chair. In fact, after their choices have hit the block you'll find them vacating their chairs en masse. That is your first hopeful sign that you have a chance. Observe the other bidders who remain. If you can separate the professional dealers from the amateurs, that will help your bidding. If one of them bids against you, you know (or can assume) he will stop when the bid is higher than he can hope to sell the object for. In other words, a Shaker chair that he can sell for one hundred and fifty dollars, he won't likely buy for a hundred. Maybe he'll stop at seventy-five.

Hunter's Tip: Don't go by the auction-catalog description. Generally a reputable auction house like Sotheby Parke-Bernet or Harmer, Rooke & Co. offers guarantees of authenticity on various antiques and relics. Others, though reputable, may not.

Because so many reproductions and fakes are around, the time is obviously at hand when all of the fine auction houses will take the time to carefully evaluate their rarities, and offer similar guarantees. Many good auction houses today still don't have such guarantees. That doesn't mean they aren't reputable. It's up to you to know what the clues are that say whether a piece is true or false—before you bid on it. It would be nice if we could take auction catalogs at face value. Realize though, the auction house is trying to be as specific as possible when they say a piece is "in the style of." It's your job to figure out if it is "in the style of" or authentic. That's one way of doing well at auctions.

It never hurts after you've attended several auctions in one gallery to let the head of the gallery know what you are looking for. Though he naturally favors the major moneyed bidders, he'll try to keep you happy, too. While these big-city auctions held in galleries tend to feature upper-bracket art and objects, they still have to get rid of many things of lesser value consigned along with the silk Tabriz. In this category are Victorian pottery, small Oriental objects, and values under one hundred dollars.

The storefront or "bare boards" auction feature pieces of furniture and collectibles that may need refinishing or repair. Here is where to find bargains. However, there is much junque to wade through. Many decorators and second-rate antique dealers show up here. The decorators are looking for quaint objet d'art like brass cash registers, English pub tables and Victorian washstands and tiles. Generally you can munch on hot dogs and coffee purchased on the premises while bidding goes on. A bit informal, but fun. To give you an example of the variables, a set of twelve, first-year editions of *Playboy* magazine took the highest bid. This is the city version of the country auction.

Auctions to avoid like leprosy or be suspicious of are those held in an empty private home or luxury apartment. Usually they are advertised as estate auctions. They may be legitimate with many fine objects that actually belong to the estate. Or, they may be "padded" with all kinds of reproductions, fakes, and junk brought in from the auction-house residue.

One such auction was held in an old suburban mansion. A friend who had been in the home during the deceased owner's lifetime was anxious to attend the auction. Imagine her surprise when she didn't recognize any of the furnishings being represented as his estate. Her bewilderment so piqued my curiosity I decided to join her on auction day.

Even though I had missed preview day the objects to be auctioned off were still scattered about, waiting for their number to come up. It offered an opportunity to check the gallery-sale catalog description against the objects. Now no person can be an expert on every single type of antique—I am no exception. My first clue as to the type of auction house this was came in the sale catalog. It stated that the gallery was in no way responsible for correctness, genuineness, period, source, origin, or condition of the objects being offered. Among the things going at auction were "antique Chinese cinnabar bowls and vases." Needless to say, the cinnabar wasn't the right color or feel for an antique. According to my friend, the late owner would never have had the overly ornate gilded Louis Quatorze *style* furnishings in the home. The Dorothy Doughty birds, however, belonged.

My most fascinating discovery was a listing for two antique pressed-glass decanters. One was an empty, circa 1967, bourbon bottle from a few Christmases ago. The other, a 1920s dime-store variety of pressed glass. Yet, later, someone paid fifty dollars for the set. I can't feel sorry for him, can you? Maybe he was carried away by auction fever. The finishing touch was a silver teapot in Georgian design, and so designated. My friend pulled me aside and whispered, "They've taken the paper label off of this. Yesterday it said 'Made in Japan.'" On the bottom were markings that a novice might take for some kind of hallmark. Naturally we couldn't wait to see who bought this genuine Georgian antique silver piece—and for how much. Sure enough the bidding was fast and furious. It ended up with two dealers bitterly battling it out for a closing bid of three hundred dollars. Did we just imagine the whole thing? Didn't the buyer look at the pieces or did he come after the paper label was removed? If so, why was he buying Georgian silver without knowing what the silversmith's marks should look like? Or, perhaps he did know and planned to sell it for twice as much to an unsuspecting buyer? Alas, I'll never know.

Hunter's Tip: Attend as many different estate auctions as you can without bidding. You'll quickly get the idea of what type of an operation it is. Observe the objects for sale. Are they mostly schlock with one or two "bait" pieces tossed in?

The practice of bringing in new pieces to estate sales is perfectly all right—if so noted in the brochure. Should you have suspicions that the estate of a spinster schoolmarm never included a pipe collection, ask the gallery supervisor right out. If he clears his throat and walks past you to greet a long-lost friend—be skeptical. Stay home and save your money for another day.

Anne Gilbert

Country auctions offer the hunter a challenge. The best time to go is not in the summer when everybody stands around in the sunshine—but in the dead of winter. You won't have as much competition on a snowy day. This doesn't apply to hunters living in warm sunny climes. But, if they are really dedicated, they'll head into the ice and snow to some country auctions. The best way to keep abreast of when and where these scattered auctions are is in publications like *Collector's Weekly*. Or, if you are planning trips to, say, Iowa or Michigan, subscribe to a small-town paper in the area you plan to be near. If you like old rope beds and other primitives, here is where to find them.

Hunter's Tip: Keep remembering what is of value to one person may not be to another.

I heard a tale recently that almost broke my heart. The elderly father of a friend decided to clean out the furnishings in his tenant-farmer dwellings and replace them with up-to-date beds, etc. He called the local auctioneer and told him to come around with a truck. On a cold November morning, so the story goes, that truck hauled away several cherry rope beds, Boston rockers, and cupboards of the same vintage. They were put up at auction early in February when the auctioneer got around to having an auction. The rope beds went for five dollars each. The cupboards from fifteen to twenty-five dollars. They were worth ten to twenty times that. In the first place there weren't many dealers at that cold auction. In fact, there was hardly anyone at all. My friend was upset that her father had cleaned up without even telling her. She even missed the auction. Miracles still happen to antique hunters. Consider the people who did attend that auction!

Not all country auctions are such winners. The majority will have lots of old toasters, toilets, and dime-store crockery. The best ones are held in someone's home, rather than a barn. Generally, if the house is worthy of a country-auction estate sale there are plenty of worthwhile antiques and collectibles lying around. Even on a winter day they will draw plenty of dealers. Perhaps they won't be interested in a single old spatter-ware bowl or art nouveau box.

Auction Hunter's Tip: Look for the antiques that aren't currently popular. Kitchen tables and single side-chairs or small pieces in Empire style (if you like the look). This is a good chance to pick up single pieces of pottery, porcelain, and glassware in a pattern you may be collecting. A glass top for your oil lamp in ruby flash might be yours for a quarter. Your own good taste and eye for form and craftsmanship can help you. Small washstands (bedside tables) with spool or turned legs turn up for a couple of dollars. Even if they need repairs or refinishing, keep in mind you'd pay fifty dollars for one in good condition. Picture frames, the beautiful old cherry ones, often go very low. Many with the prints or family likenesses still in them. Sadly the velvet-covered family albums are expensive and gobbled up by wise dealers.

If you have done your homework the best is yet to come. Can you recognize a Queen Anne or Sheraton leg, even under coats of paint? A jelly cupboard covered with thick layers of paint? Here is where you may be lucky. Most dealers don't want to have to get into a lot of refinishing and repairs. On a cold winter's eve they are even less likely to want to lug one back to the shop. A little elbow grease on your part can turn a five-dollar cupboard into one worth over a hundred— and a handsome antique for your home. Give those heavily camouflaged pieces a second glance. Don't be surprised at finding Southern antiques or Eastern antiques at a Midwestern country auction. People and things travel. Anything can happen.

There are many cutesy antique shopping centers (I don't know what else to call them) that are in farm communities near large cities. A couple of hours drive and you are transplanted to historic Crudsville featuring twelve antique shops, two restaurants, and a sweet shoppe. These man-made tourist traps have been popping up during the last fifteen years. Prices are sky high. But, who cares when the atmosphere is quaint. They are usually built around some historic building. First, the townsfolk band together to save one or two "landmarks." They are followed by a few architects or the nucleus of a small creative group, with sincere motives and a love of historic lifestyle. The first thing you know, word spreads that this is a site for reviving an entire Victorian community. Ye Olde Inn is followed by what else but antique shops. A restaurant opens with waitresses in Victorian and Colonial costumes and it becomes the center of activity. Not only does it offer country-style dining, but an auction once or twice a week. The public is invited to bring things to sell or to come and bid. Taking it one step further, everything in sight, except the waitress, is for sale. Busloads of ladies' luncheon groups are carted out for a day or evening of shopping and dining. Wouldn't you think this would be a peachy spot to find real antiques at auction? Visions of elderly farmers cleaning out barns and attics and plunking down the contents on auction night dance like visions of sugar plums in antique hunters' heads. But, let's sit in on auction night. Friendly Colonel Tiddledywinks, dressed in Kentucky Colonel fashion, is the auctioneer. Of course, good hunter that you are, you view the items to be auctioned before the event. What do you see? Ten copper coal buckets with Delft handles, fresh from the wholesale house; reproductions of atrocious floral-painted oil lamps (one three-feet tall); cut glass of every shape, straight from East Germany and Poland; reproductions of brass and rubber automobile horns; and the prize of the evening—a wooden wall-telephone, about a week old.

On with the bidding. A table of young marrieds decides to bid on a couple of the coal scuttles. The bidding goes up to forty-five dollars. One lucky person gets the bid. Another exactly like it goes for thirty-five dollars. They could be purchased for less in the local gift or flower shop. The monstrous oil lamp appeals to another couple at the same table. Yep, they've caught auction fever. But what a way to catch it. I find the impulse to bid on an old clothes wringer irresistible. It's mine for around three dollars. Two chicken-hatchery hanging lights (green metal shades) are mine for a dollar.

I must admit it was all great fun—and at least for me not too costly. The big surprise was the overpriced reproductions—and the fact that the buyers weren't aware or didn't care that they had paid too much. But, in the spirit of fun I guess it doesn't matter until the next morning anyhow.

The eat-and-buy-antiques gimmick isn't really new for restaurants. It's just that it is becoming the "in" thing for medium-priced restaurants that want to attract a new group of customers who will become regulars. Can the eager antiques and collectibles hunter find his or her thing? The merchandise in most places leans heavily on popular collectibles and Eastlake-style Victorian furniture. Ad tins and chamber pots do lend a certain air to dining. Nothing like a brass headboard or giant Coca-Cola tin hanging precariously over your head. Generally the collectibles are high priced—higher than shop prices. Should a hunter bother looking? Absolutely. The element of chance makes anything possible. In such a place I found my second Shaker chair—hanging on a wall. At first I didn't pay any attention. After all, who'd expect to find an early nineteenth-century Shaker chair in the heart of a Midwestern city? Munching on a gourmetburger I happened to notice the walnut splint chair seat. Taking a closer look I observed the Shaker-design finials and the score lines. The seat was a fan shape, lending additional grace to the chair. And, the price tag was an unbelievable twenty-two dollars. Without further ado, I grabbed it off the wall before it disappeared. I asked one of the managers how the store came by the chair.

"Oh, I found it at a block sale around the corner," he said. Shaker in the city—at what used to be country prices, long, long ago. Unfortunately, that was the only unusual find in the restaurant. But who knows, you may discover a bargain.

Warehouse sales used to be an exciting way to find antiques. Sometimes you just bid on a large trunk; contents unknown. Other times you bid on items you can see. There is an element of excitement in opening a packing crate that has been practically forgotten by its owners for fifty years. Or, the owner has died and the heirs want to get rid of the storage items—and the bill. Many warehouses sell these leftovers in an adjacent warehouse, in retail fashion. Sadly, the items are usually priced as high as shop prices. Unless you know absolutely what you are doing, you may be paying far more for an antique than you would in a shop. Everybody is into the antiques craze. Like the auctions, some warehouse sales are "padded." But you wouldn't be fooled into buying something new that merely appears old.

Container sales have been around a long time, but I don't think too many hunters are aware of them. These are really a game of chance—not only for the dealer-buyer, but the antique hunter. Most of the merchandise is ordered sight unseen by the dealers from a warehouse in Antwerp, Belgium, or various countries. The Belgium warehouse circulates furniture and bric-a-brac from Europe, and parts of Asia. The dealer may either visit the warehouse and order from things he sees—or, without seeing. He may specify he wants furniture, china, etc. Where does it come from? Pickers go out and scour second-hand shops for likely objects. What is a likely object? Not necessarily an antique. Rather objects that would be classified as second-hand furniture; not old enough to be antique. But, different enough in style to be passed off as an antique. How many antique hunters would be familiar with department store furniture from Berlin, or Antwerp? This type of selling has been going on for thirty years or more. Doubtless by now some of the things are antiques. What is the destination of the container objects? Shopping-center auctions, country auctions, and flea markets, as well as some small dealers. There is nothing dishonest in this type of buying and selling and sometimes you may come up with a winner. The dealer can always say he doesn't know any more about what he bought than the customer. And it's the truth. For a long time I've been curious about the flood of so-called antiques that are furnishing the flourishing giant antique-selling centers. After all, there were only so many objects created several hundred years ago. There are more now than then. There are many of these closed "container" sales to choose from. One advertises "hundreds of containers unloaded at our New Orleans Docks daily." A firm called British Antique Exporters Ltd. services the New Orleans docks. The containers are auctioned at dockside. The same firm will ship directly to you, to your nearest dock. If you would like to play this game of chance, mail for their catalog, at New Road Industrial Estate, New Haven, Sussex, England.

Container Hunter's Tip: If you can't readily identify a style or type of antique at a follow-up auction, where you can see the contents—be wary. The pieces may just be an unusual European design made a few years ago—commonplace department store furniture in Ireland or Scotland—but new to our shores.

Of course, since many of the things are bought at estate sales abroad, you might even find a valuable early American antique. If you can afford it, buy a couple of containers, pick through them. You can always hold your own auction and get rid of the "junque."

If you like giant amusement parks your happiness is secure with the opening in Florida (between Disney World and Orlando) of Antique World. One of the features is six auctions a week scheduled with shipments of antiques arriving constantly from Europe and Asia. Sounds like the ideal stopping-off place for those container-sale items that also, by chance, arrive coast to coast daily. So, you see, if you somehow miss buying these guessing-game antiques in your neck of the woods, you can find them on your Florida vacation.

What would you say to paying one hundred and thirty dollars for a reproduction of an antique hall stand with a mirror, fifty-five dollars for a pendulum clock, or sixty-three dollars for a small washstand—all unpainted? Yes, some enterprising soul has come up with a line of brand-new, unpainted antique repros of some popular styles. They are advertised as hard to find and easy to finish. There is a piano stool with swivel seat for seventy-four dollars and a corner five-tier what-not shelf for seventy-two dollars. Not including your stain or finish and labor, this has to cost the buyer twice as much as the real thing. Yes, as you now are aware, you can still find any of these authentic pieces with a little effort. The piano stool could be yours for from twenty-five to fifty dollars; washstands from four dollars up, and so on. Give a thought to the fact that in a few years even these unpainted pieces will become sufficiently battered to be sold to the innocent, uninformed buyer at antique prices. Probably at auction.

Hardware stores, pet shops, and florists are all getting into the antique-selling act. A couple of hardware stores shamelessly mix reproductions with their few country antiques—at higher than bona fide dealer prices.

Hunter's Tip: Go to as many types of auctions and sales as possible. Observe and compare. After a while, just as in darkness, your eyes will grow accustomed to objects that are overpriced and reproduced. It costs nothing to look.

Many of the finest auction houses and most worthwhile auctions will send you a catalog of objects being auctioned at their next one. Cost of the catalog from two dollars up. Even if you can't attend, you can check what some of the items go for in the various antiques publications. The follow-up stories can then be recorded in your auction catalog. An invaluable reference for several reasons. You may be amazed at the amount of "rare" Queen Anne or Chippendale or Georgian silver that shows up repeatedly at auctions around the country. This might lead you to assume that some are not what they purport to be. It also helps you keep track of trends in popularity of antiques and collectibles.

Consider that for many years Indian art and Victorian paintings were rarely seen at auction. If so, they didn't fetch much of a price. Now, Indian and Western art is going for phenomenal prices and Victorian paintings are on the upsurge. By knowing what the trends are, you might possibly sell off a popular object that you don't care for, and make a profit. Use your money to invest in the things you collect.

Pawing through pawnshops is an experience no true hunter can afford to miss. When you've "done all the U.S. pawnshops" you still have hunting grounds in Europe awaiting you. Let's start visiting the big-city pawnbrokers and working our way down. While I can't say for sure, I will venture a guess that there are hundreds of pawnshops in even the smaller cities. If you want to really do it right, you could probably go through the yellow pages or classified phone books, coast to coast. Make out lists and systematically visit them.

Probably because of the nature of the business, most pawnshops are located in older or sleazy business districts. Don't let that bother you. Instead, let it add an element of adventure to your hunting. Who knows, you may even get mugged!

Who goes to pawnshops these days? What do they pawn? Jewelry is still the number-one pawnable, followed by guitars. You'd be amazed at how many guitars are in pawnshops all over the country. In fact, some shops sell them as a sideline. War medals and silver are a close third and fourth. Not interested? Then break it down further, into old, long-established pawnshops or new ones. Skip the new ones. They usually avoid the type of things their grandfathers took in. Many of the older shops still have pawned items dating to the turn of the century.

Now you can't hope to beat a pawnbroker (usually) out of jewelry. That is one of his specialties. Hopefully, there will be some odd items like Art Deco cigarette cases or Victorian beaded bags with silver frames. An occasional small piece of furniture, long forgotten, may be in the pawnbroker's storeroom. The sincere hunter will sniff about first, then ask.

Prices will be high for things the pawnbroker values. That may not be what you are looking for. The hand-painted napkin ring that will be a unique addition to your collection may be a couple of dollars. How about a solid-ivory billiard ball for ten dollars—even if you don't play the game?

You might as well know that the pawnbroker has a regular clientele of antique dealers. Your only hope is to come in on a day before they do or be looking for objects that don't interest them. The kitsch hunter can do very well in pawnshops. There are always a couple of elks' teeth, buttonhooks, and curling irons in pawn-shop cabinets. What value do they have, you may ask. What will you pay?

Many pawnbrokers buy their own pieces at auctions and private sales—the same place you do. It stands to reason the pawnshop prices on these items will be higher than their auction or housesale prices. This puts the hunter right back where he started from—at the housesales. But, there is always the chance of recogniz-ing something that a pawnbroker doesn't.

Even suburban street fairs offer the hunter oppor-tunities. It is all a matter of "Kismet."

How about a sixteenth-century silver candelabrum for four dollars and fifty cents? A lucky friend found exactly that at a suburban street fair, sponsored by the village. For some reason, the dealers hadn't expected to come across a silver antique candelabrum—and had passed it by.

Hunter's Tip: Expect the unexpected. Anything can hap-pen at a large sale or a small one. Obviously, you have as good a chance as the dealers if you can make a spot judgment—and the price is low enough.

This nineteenth-century quilt was a reject at a country auction in Milford, Indiana. That isn't a Nazi emblem but a popular quilt pattern. It is in perfect condition: dark blue bent cross against a white ground. I was excited to get it for four dollars and fifty cents several years ago. Quilts of this vintage are getting quite costly, running into the hundreds of dollars in the shops. Once in a while, you can still find one at a private house sale for twenty-five dollars. In fact, dealers are even buying up badly damaged quilts of good designs. They are often chopped up for pillows and small framed wall hangings. You might consider doing the same.

The ultimate happiness for the antique hunter—dining under the wheels of an old buggy. Hopefully, it is securely attached to the ceiling. If it isn't, what a way to go! Please note, everything in this restaurant can be yours—for a price. Many items are on consignment. Others have been purchased by the owner. Who knows what you can find? After all, presumably the owner and staff are busy as restaurateurs—not antique experts. As a result, they may have some valuable antique priced low. You'd better believe the owner knows about Tiffany and that lamp is priced accordingly.

A cozy spot for two in front of the old Victorian hat rack. Which you can buy—after you've eaten. Remember the old days when you took a date to a restaurant and a little old lady selling flowers would stop by? You'd buy your date a flower! Now your date takes you to Ye Olde Pine Cupboard and she buys you an old advertising tin, or an old iron shoe last.

'Twas the night before bidding and all through the auction house not a creature was stirring—but wait. An elegant array of antiques has been on display. The wise hunter will have leisurely browsed amongst them, carefully examining objects he intends to bid on. Miracles do happen, even at quality auction houses like this one. A sleeper may be waiting for your educated eye.

—*Courtesy*: Chicago Art Gallery

Elegant authentic antiques like these can be found at auction—for a price. Many times a wealthy collector will send his representative to bid on an object. Instructions will state the amount he can bid up to. The only chance you have is that few bidders are interested—or that you have saved your money for this event. Shown are: *A Social Gathering*, oil painting, Dutch school, eighteenth century; Chippendale mahogany armchair with center open design band with separate cushion seat, circa 1760; antique Georgian mahogany small circular tripod table, circa 1780; and Chippendale mahogany armchair with cross-ribbon back, circa 1780.

—*Courtesy*: Chicago Art Gallery

Nautical antiques and collectibles are popular auction items. Many times they are parts of collections. Or, they might be status objects from the *Queen Mary* or *Ile de France*. Who could resist buying a porthole for several hundred dollars or some plumbing fixtures from a famous ship? Many hunters find this type of collectible irresistable.

—*Courtesy*: Chicago Art Gallery

Figural bottles are among the most eagerly sought items for bottle collectors. "Santa," is probably a German bottle, late nineteenth century. Some of the original paint is still intact. The Indian Empress Bitters bottle replica in clear glass is thought to have been made in Italy a few years ago. It was on the top shelf of a resale shop priced for seven dollars. Recently I sold it and traded with another bottle collector for considerably more. The soldier on the right was found in a shop in Massachusetts for six dollars. It is probably European. So far I haven't seen its duplicate or a listing in any of the bottle guides.

Thrift shops take in all kinds of things. Careful hunting may turn up an addition to your antique goblet collection for a couple of dollars. This early pressed-glass goblet has a "flashed" top border. Thrift shops are also good places to fill in missing pieces of silver, china, and glassware.

Cutesy collectibles like this washboard with floral decor, gas iron, and old wringer are best-sellers in city restaurants where antiques are on the menu.

These collectibles aren't old enough to be antiques. They fall in a class all by themselves as decorator collectibles. For some reason, they are considered great for office decor. A wall of old washboards, or a wringer here and an iron there, can really dress up those file cabinets. The washboards range from four to fifteen dollars. The deciding factor is the wood advertising section. From twelve dollars up is a going wringer rate. The gasoline-iron ranges go from eight dollars up.

Now your handy neighborhood hardware store is "into" antiques. The only trouble is, they don't really qualify as antiques. Mostly, you'll find golden oak and hundreds of reproductions of Victorian-art glasses and pressed glass. Sometimes, some hardware store wrought-iron items are casually mixed in with the antiques. After all, lots of people don't know what you do. The prize at this antique "shoppe" was an old wooden wash tub with wringer for a mere one hundred fifty dollars. Don't rush in. By now the price has probably gone up.

Antique shops specializing in collectibles are fun to shop in. And, a good place to look for unrecognized early antiques. The owner often has to buy in quantity to acquire a single collectible that he really wants. You may recognize an early Oriental dish or spot a nineteenth-century pine cupboard priced low here. By the same token, because his values are different, the gum-ball machines may cost one hundred or more dollars. If you think you've seen everything, poke around a shop like this. Such fun things as a penny arcade, "girlie" machine or a "shoot Hitler" machine are for sale— and trying out.

Double dips for salt are some of the unusual "cheapies" hunters may spot in auction house box-lots. The "owl" dip on the right was found at a small shop in Paris. The other, from an auction box-lot from a country auction.

Handpainted china pieces are dependent on their designers good taste. China painting began in England. The first classes in America were taught by an Englishman, Edward Lycett, after the Civil War. Designs of this period were Moorish and Persian. By 1900, china painting was one of the most popular young ladies' crafts. Many books were published on the subject. The books themselves would certainly be a collector's item today. If you can believe statistics, there were over twenty thousand of these amateur painters by 1905.

Golden oak is a big seller in hardware-antique stores, country antique shops, and instant-antique villages. Prices range from two hundred fifty to four hundred fifty dollars for this cabinet-desk-bookcase. This one was found for eighty-five dollars and refinished by the owner before the golden oak craze. The design won a prize at the 1893 Columbian Exposition. Hundreds were produced and even sold. Many were similar, but not exact copies of the "winner." Young people appreciate its multi-purpose storage space and small scale. Keep looking if you like it. As I said, there were plenty of them.
—*Courtesy*: Mrs. J. L. Jasper

7
Separating Ducks from Decoys—and Other Quackery

IN ANTIQUE HUNTING no one is an expert. That includes me. It also includes dealers, collectors, and museum curators. Some are more knowledgeable than others. Remember in antique hunting there can always be an exception to the rule. Perhaps there is one Chippendale chair or one piece of Paul Revere silver that hasn't been cataloged and recorded. Perhaps because it is different than the norm associated with the period it has gone undetected and unloved for a couple of hundred years. In antique hunting anything can happen—and be discovered. Because not everyone can be well versed on all phases the burden falls on you and me to know all we can about what interests us most. Otherwise, regardless of how much money you spend, or how reputable the authority who sells you an antique, it may not be what it purports to be. Don't blame it on the dealer if your Queen Anne lowboy was made yesterday. Perhaps he doesn't know either.

The reason many people buy reproductions as antiques is because most of us are lazy. It is easier to accept somebody's word that an object is old—rather than research it in the library. It would be delightful if you could just walk into a shop or housesale and get the correct answer about everything on sale. Actually many of the sellers aren't purposely dishonest. It takes many years and much research to become at all skilled in recognizing the genuine article. And, it takes a questioning mind. What happened the last time you went into a very posh antique shop to look at a beautiful country cupboard . . . did you take the dealer's word as you plunked down several hundred dollars? Or, did you ask to see the back of it, and to examine the inside and bottom? If you are a serious customer, no honest dealer would object to careful scrutiny. It takes great courage to question. And, unless you study up, you have no business hunting antiques . . . or questioning a dealer.

Some people would say, "What difference does it make if a piece is a reproduction, if you have a paper of authentication?"

The difference becomes quite important when you in turn try to sell that antique at auction. Believe me, the professional collectors, dealers, and auction people aren't timid about visually taking apart an antique. And they aren't about to be impressed by that little paper until they prove to their satisfaction the piece is authentic.

If it isn't, you will have a piece of second-hand furniture, worth the price of second-hand furniture. It will have decreased in price. The genuine antique would have increased.

This failing of the human nature, to really check and double-check, is what gives all of us amateurs a fighting chance to discover beautiful things for bargain prices.

Reproductions are so rampant these days in everything from antique jewelry to Oriental pieces it becomes almost a challenge for the hunter to guess which is which. Some manufacturers are turning out instant art nouveau jewelry, silver, and you name it. You, too, could market art nouveau jewelry. Since none of the pieces were copyrighted originally, all you need is some of the original jewelry molds and somebody to put it all together. Some sellers are very blatant about it. They advertise in antique publications to the attention of the dealer only. The unscrupulous dealers or would-be dealers can order the catalog of fakes, and presto! at the next antique show dozens of art nouveau pieces are offered at enormous prices to the unsuspecting.

Recently I went to a reputable jeweler who was kind enough to show me his trade catalog offering "antique type slides and chains." The price, without precious stones, in gold fill ran from fifteen dollars and up. He then showed me some of the pieces. It was hard to believe they hadn't been rescued from a Victorian attic. He sells them as new. But, who's to say what another less honest would do. A talented Israeli is creating them. But not to fool the public.

The Oriental Art Collectors' Club has been warning its members as of late about the flood of "tomb" figures showing up, as well as porcelain in blue and white. They are represented as being "antique." The prices are high, but not high enough for what they are supposed to be.

Recently a friend of mine proudly showed me a "Ming" horse tomb-figure she had purchased from a reputable dealer. She paid several hundred dollars. It came with a paper authenticating it as a genuine Ming horse. There was even burial clay on its base.

The price was the first clue. A genuine Ming horse would be priced in the thousands. Let's face it, no dealer is about to be this generous—even for a good customer. Naturally, my friend was enraged that I had suggested such a thing. Finally she agreed to take it to a collector who was a specialist in Ming. He pointed out that it was made in the 1890s or early 1900s. There was great interest in tomb excavations at that time and the Chinese took advantage of the fact. Lots of "tomb" figures were discovered in shops in the 1900s. In a book called *Fakes* by Otto Kurz, he reports visiting a factory in Peking at that time and seeing hundreds being made. As for my friend, she still wouldn't believe. She took it to two museum curators with the same result. The problem with her—and most of us who have been had—is believing. We don't want to believe we have bought a dud.

The head of a large auction gallery once told me not only had he bought fakes as the real thing, but just about everyone does. The important thing, he noted, is not to make the same mistakes again.

Just to make you feel better I was taken in by a bottle. Pre-1900 bottles and figurals are my thing. And, when I can find one cheaply, I collect whisky flasks from 1850 to 1870. My collection began about fifteen years ago when I bought some antique bottles at a country auction. One of my next purchases was a Jenny Lind bottle that a dealer assured me was old. It had a pontil mark on the bottom, but not a rough one. In my innocence, it never occurred to me it was a reproduction. However, I began searching for it in the bottle catalogs. Years later I found it listed in a book of reproductions. It had been made in Czechoslovakia in the 1900s. Did that stop me from searching for bottle bargains? Nope. On the whole I did rather well. At a housesale, I picked up three genuine historical flasks. The dealers had passed them by because they weren't sure, and thought they were reproductions. By this time, I knew enough about bottles and reproductions. I was sure the bottles were authentic, and they were. Mine for six dollars and three dollars. But, suddenly I became the big expert. I let my overconfidence get the best of me. At a very fancy antique show I felt certain I had discovered a rare South Jersey bottle for twenty-five dollars. I did everything wrong. I asked the dealer what she knew about it. She assured me it was old and from the East. I could see for myself the rough pontil and the bubbles. Everything looked right. But, there was no descriptive listing in my reference books. The rude awakening came when I saw my bottle being offered in an advertisement at a Texas antique show for "five dollars for the first thirty that buy tickets for two." It was indeed from the East. The ad further stated "this early Persian camel saddle bottle *similar* to those made in 1700, etc." I had visions of a factory of Persians blowing them out for the suckers . . . just like me. Since then I have seen it at other shows priced up to thirty-five dollars. I can't resist asking the sellers about it. Invariably they reply—it's very old—from the East. And, of course, the imagination runs wild—to thoughts of South Jersey.

Silver is another object often reproduced. One of my favorite shops offers nothing but reproductions, sold as such. Silver, china, just about any small popular antique, can be found here in reproduced form. There are Matthew Boulton, Harrison and Hobson, Sheffield. Pieces from Queen Anne to Queen Victoria. Some of them are put out by a company called Regal Reproductions. They aren't being made to really fool anybody. Yet, here again, many of the unscrupulous are having a profitable picnic with silver repros. There are hundreds of silver marks. Unless you are pretty well-read or know your dealer, you can be had. Victorian silver napkin rings at very high prices are popular at the current shows. Are they old or new? It's up to you to know before you buy—not after.

I religiously follow the column by Mr. Jabe Tartar in a publication called *Collector's Weekly*. He writes about the reproduction-of-the-week and tells how they're doing it. One column told about newly made platform rockers being buried in manure for several months to "age them." Think about that one for a few minutes.

Not all reproductions are of the inexpensive variety. Auffray & Co. proudly advertises the "Ancienne Boiserie" collection of armoires, secretaries, and a bibliotheca of items made of antique woods, old hardware, and hinges. Can't you see some dishonest dealer asking twice as much as the furniture manufacturer for his "authentic pieces"? Of course, you and I would know better, wouldn't we? The smart thing to do is buy a piece at its furniture store price and fool your snooty friends.

There's nothing wrong with buying a reproduction if you don't pay antique prices. Remember there is hardly an object of design merit that hasn't been reproduced. The smart antique hunter makes sure the piece has five or more positive antique features before he buys. Or, consider collecting reproductions.

American primitives are the up-and-coming popular

antiques. Wouldn't you think that there would be plenty of authentic corner cupboards and pine beds lying around without having to fake any? I hate to tell you but in the 1920s, American country pieces became the "in" antiques. It was terribly chic to furnish an otherwise sophisticated city apartment with primitives. As more people started hunting, more fakes were created to meet the needs. With due process of aging consider how those 1920 fakes have weathered some fifty years later—to a beautiful, mellow patina.

The 1920 fakers put lots of "knots" in their pieces. Supposedly this would be the finishing touch of authenticity. Several years ago, I bought one of these 1920 fakes—a pine bed. The knot holes were beautifully evident. Unfortunately, the last thing the early craftsmen would do would be to use a piece with knot holes in it. As the wood would age, expanding and contracting, the knots would fall out. So, don't let anyone tell you that "knotty pine" with knots is the real thing.

In the early days when there was plenty of wood around, the artisans could be choosy. They wouldn't need to use just any old piece. They could use the wood for the beauty of its grain, especially those pieces from the center of the logs.

How far back in history does the faking of antiques go? As far back as history. But, in our more recent past 1906 apparently was a very good year for making instant antiques. In a quote from a February, 1906, *Good Housekeeping*, the article stated that about 90 percent of the things sold as antiques "are bogus."

"In ways that are dark and tricks that are vain, and lucrative, the heathen Chinese was never so peculiar as the dealers in antiques. Almost everyone of them has

103

in his back room or basement anywhere from half a dozen to a score of workmen busy manufacturing antique furniture."

Going back to the 1870s, the fakers were busy in factories devoted strictly to forgeries in some of the major cities in Europe. A popular item was the Gothic cupboard. Now, move forward to the 1970s and note the periodic appearance in the finest shops, heralding "a fine gothic cupboard" for several thousand dollars. Is it or isn't it?

In the 1800s French furniture was being reproduced in great quantity. Has it aged well? Have you just bought a piece as an investment?

The only note of hope for all of this is that by now all of these thousands of forgeries in furniture, porcelain, and glass will probably pass undetected for the rest of history. So, perhaps that Gothic cabinet is a good investment after all. The moral of the story must surely be to be certain your fakes are *old* fakes.

Dealers Can Be Hunting Casualties, Too

Despite my somewhat jaded attitude toward antique dealers, I must admit there are many whose opinions I often solicit. Sometimes they know the answers. Sometimes they don't. And, sometimes they too can be had by a trickster. The antiquing world is a small one and slowly the word gets around that there is a wolf loose amongst the lambs. Can you imagine the rage of dealers who discover another dealer has been palming off fakes on them?

An elderly dealer who prides herself on authentic and good antiques (no nostalgia stuff here) was visibly unnerved. It seemed she had purchased some silhouettes and other small pieces from a couple of come-lately dealers. By mere chance an artist specializing in silhouettes had spotted the silhouettes in her shop window. Much to the elderly dealer's surprise the woman announced she had made them. She specialized in copying museum-piece silhouettes, and had sold quite a few, in all innocence, to the young dealers for five dollars each. The dealers had charged the elderly dealer sixty-five dollars and up for them, as authentic pieces. When the elderly woman charged the couple with cheating her and demanded her money back, they told her she should know more about antiques. It was her own fault. After making a few phone calls, she discovered others had been buying from the couple. Meanwhile, what can anyone do? Will the dealers throw out the crooks—bar them from antique shows? Or, will they go their merry way laughing all the way to the bank?

Backtracking a little I found the dealers hadn't bothered to remove the backs from the silhouettes before purchase. They had assumed the pictures were authentic. When dealers can fool dealers that's really getting rough. What chance do you have? Plenty, if you remember to take the back off the silhouette before you plunk down that cash. You would discover they were done on new paper, not even with age spots.

However, there is a small bit of justice. I've been told another deal who had been cheated by the pair got revenge. When they drove up with a van filled with hundreds of small antiques and furniture, she let them take out each piece and go through their sales pitch. After which she told them she wasn't buying that day.

Keeping in mind that "dealers" can be had too, I have figured out some hunter's techniques that netted me a

Anne Gilbert

couple of Oriental art objects at a bargain price. Since many dealers specialize in a period or a type of antique or collectible they are naturally well-versed in their specialties. The dealer who collects advertising tins and painted porcelain may be just the one to sell you a Chinese blue-and-white piece cheaply. The reasoning is simple. What he is interested in is of more value to him than what he doesn't collect. Often he may have had to buy many antiques he isn't interested in in order to acquire the pieces he covets. In one shop specializing in advertising collectibles, I came across a blue-and-white porcelain bowl and a blue-and-white ginger jar, priced under twenty dollars apiece. The dealer explained that he had acquired them along with some Coca-Cola tins and a spool cabinet. They had been gathering dust for several years. At the same time a very large shallow bowl in a blue-and-white Oriental design was priced at around fifty dollars. The dealer had been told the large bowl was "old," and that it did have a "mark" on it. Since Oriental antiques weren't his thing, the dealer couldn't tell that the large bowl was circa 1973, and the mark was fake. It was currently selling for twelve dollars in Oriental gift shops. The porcelain dish was early nineteenth century and the ginger jar the same period.

How do reproductions manage to find their way into private collections? One way is when they are first planted in barns and country shops, waiting for you to "discover" them. A well-known book on the subject of fakes was written by the late early American glass expert, Ruth Webb Lee. In *Antique Fakes & Reproductions*, she tells about pickers and runners who planted reproductions of early American whisky flasks and South Jersey bottles with farmers in the 1930s. Some pieces came from Czechoslovakia and Mexico. Have times changed? I doubt it.

The popularity of old wall clocks and tall-case (grandfather's) clocks has led to importing on a giant scale from Germany. Are they just made or actually antiques? When you see advertisements of "500 German tall cases arriving monthly from the continent" it makes you a tiny bit suspicious. That would mean an awful lot of people had once owned these clocks. At this rate, more clocks than people existed at that time. Equally curious is another advertisement of antique clocks from the Orient, "mostly Japanese made; all pre-1945 and some German made pre-1910." The illustrations I saw are similar to our popular school wall-clock. In both cases, dealers are invited to buy in quantity.

What would make you think one of these clocks is old? According to a friend who has seen them, they are well-aged. They are often made from old clock parts. The cases are made from picture molding and old wood.

Hunter's Tip: Read the ads in the various newspapers and trade publications for antique buyers and sellers. You'll be able to trace the arrival of a shipment of phonies in Columbia, Indiana, to your dealer's doorstep, when he runs his ad in the Slobovia Gazette.

Many publications like *Hobbies* won't take ads of this type. However, I wish they would. That is one of the ways we can all be alerted to the reproductions soon to appear at the next antique show or in our local shops. If all of this information does nothing for the skeptics who feel all is peachy in the antique world—it should at least pique their curiosity.

A popular fake flask made in the twentieth century—this Jenny Lind bottle. The pontil on the bottom is smooth and machine made. The light-yellow color was not found on the original. This probably was made in Czechoslovakia in quantity. Then it was planted in shops and barns all over the United States for collectors "to discover."

This facsimile of Moses-at-the-Spring bottle sells at flea markets and antique shows for eight dollars and up. It is green, and was filled with gin when it was for sale about six years ago. Filled, it cost around five dollars. The original is a scarce item. The first repro was made in the early 1900s in clear glass and contained water from the Poland Mineral Springs.

Sometimes you can spot a whole new world of fakes bursting into the antique market—by reading the ads. For months this advertisement catering to dealers appeared in antiques publications coast to coast. I came across the belt buckle, at a street fair, for five dollars in pewter. The same buckle popped up in the famous art nouveau design at several country antique shops, and a city antique show or two—for up to fifteen dollars. Hopefully, collectors of art nouveau had read the same ads and resisted their buying impulses.

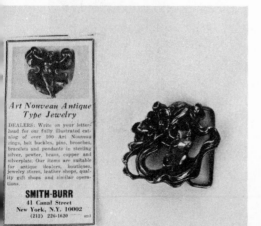

Did you buy this camel-saddle bottle for what it really is—or for what the seller told you it was? The rough pontil, imperfections, and rigaree (applied bands of glass in parallel vertical lines) made it appear at first glance to be early American glass. It was used as give-aways at a Texas antique show, and possibly others, for five dollars. It was truthfully advertised at the Texas show. After that, strange things happened—including the price going up to thirty-five dollars. By then buyers were told it was "old and from the East." How old is old—and is East really East? It now is dignified with a price guide listing of twenty-five dollars, as a Persian camel-saddle bottle.

Is it "old" Imari, fairly "old" or made yesterday? There is always a goodly supply of "Imari type" porcelain at the flea market. It is up to you to tell whether it feels and looks like the authentic pieces.

At first glance you might think this was an early Chinese blue-and-white bottle. It is properly primitive and has a small chip in one corner. The clue to its later vintage is the checkerboard design. As is, this piece sold in a shop for sixty dollars. It probably was recently exported from Taiwan and the identifying seal lost or removed in the process. Also remember, "old" to the Western world isn't the same bowl of rice as "old" to the Orientals. Chances are, these are being made at this very moment on an assembly line basis. Or, maybe it really is "old," like 1900.

Cinnabar is the faker's delight. The process of applying successive layers of vermilion lacquer and then carving out a design has been done in China for centuries. Many eighteenth-century vases and boxes were brought to the United States over the years. Close examination will give you a feeling for the early pieces. Many pieces were made in the 1920s and exported. Currently, plastic objects are being sold as old cinnabar at some "tricky" auctions. They have a bright orange appearance and not the delicacy of design of even the 1920s pieces. Beware. Cinnabar boxes like the one on the right, with the jade medallion, are priced at one hundred forty-five dollars retail. Tough luck if you pay that for a phony. The box on the left dates from the nineteenth century. It was found at a garage sale for three dollars. The box with the jade medallion was twenty dollars in a resale shop. Considering it's current value, you can say it was a "find."

Is nothing sacred? The insect boot jack on the right is a reproduction. Another popular boot-jack repro is known as "Naughty Nellie." She is an undraped female figure in iron. So far there are enough shoe lasts around that they haven't been reproduced. Or have they? They are popular flea-market sale items from three dollars up. The boot jack can run from six dollars up depending on the whim of the seller.

Glass swans in pressed glass so far aren't popular enough to be faked. Or are they? The black swan has risen in value, according to the price guides, to sixty-five dollars. Unfortunately, not many people seem to want it at that price. At least that is what the dealers tell me who are stuck with them. Swans aren't as popular as the early pressed-glass and milk-glass nested-fowl dishes.

How can you tell if milk glass is fake? Best way is to find it yourself, stored in someone's attic. The other way is to hold it to the light. Much of it will have a slight opalescence at the edges. The small lacy plate was found for a couple of dollars in a shop specializing in nostalgia and kitsch. The salt-and-pepper shakers came from a collector's home for three dollars. Both have the desired opalescence when held to the light.

Looks like an early pine rope bed doesn't it? It was purchased as an authentic piece for thirty-five dollars. Chances are it is a 1920s reproduction, made to deceive. The knot holes are not found in early country pieces. The cabinet makers knew better. As wood expands and dries out and contracts, the knotholes would eventually fall out. But, to a novice collector, the knothole has an authentic look.

There was a time when these Chinese clay figurines could be picked up in any Chinese gift shop or flea market for one dollar fifty cents to three dollars fifty cents. They were a specialty made for export in a village near Canton, China, called Buddha Mountain. They were exported before 1940 from China. Today, they cost from six dollars to thirty-five dollars for the larger sizes—and are made in Taiwan and Hong Kong. The ones you want have the word "China" imprinted in the clay. These originals had hands and faces of unglazed clay with minute details. The costumes were brightly glazed in greens, blues, yellows, and browns. Some will be fishing, others playing chess, or pouring tea. The hands are made separately to coordinate the activities.

Hunter's Tip: You can often find the old figures of smaller variety in planters, fishbowls, and the large glass bowls used in the 1930s for bottled gardens.
—Courtesy: Mrs. Walter Sobel

8

Psyching Out Antiques and Collectibles

Case History 1

LUCKY YOU—JUST found an old chest and a blue-and-white Oriental porcelain box. At least you think the box looks Oriental. The chest cost you fifteen dollars and the strong backs of your son and a friend; plus a six pack of their favorite brew. The box was a dollar and fifty cents. You found the pieces at two separate house-sales. While everybody was going through the house, fighting off dealers for golden oak and a collection of R. S. Prussia, you headed straight for the garage. There, among the potty chair, broken games, and old paperbacks, stood the chest of drawers. With its dirt and dark mahogany stain it wasn't exactly the kind of piece to fight over. Besides it was topped with an ungainly mirror attached to the back. The frame was devoid of carving. The knobs were broad, round, and wooden. One was missing. Also, a piece of one of the canted feet had broken off. What then would make this object worth a six pack of beer and the grumbling of two teenagers—let alone fifteen dollars?

Obviously something at first glance gives a clue to this dull discovery.

Clue 1—Acanthus leaf carving on each side of the chest. This was a popular motif for American Empire furniture from 1815 to 1830.

Clue 2—Dark mahogany finish. Probably this was original finish. If so, the piece could logically be Empire. This was typical stained finish of the period.

Discrepancies—The base of the piece had canted or chamfered bracket feet and scalloped apron. This was used in the 1800s and earlier.

Clue 3—The drawers were hand-dovetailed both front and back. They were uneven—four on the one drawer, five on another. Definitely made by hand. The back and front dovetailing established it as before 1830. The overlapping top drawer is Empire design.

Discrepancies—It appeared to be a "country" piece. Since it took several years for a fashion trend to go from city to country, it might have been made later.

Taking the piece out into the light you look into the drawers for labels—and at the back for signatures. None show up. You do this while waiting for the "movers." Meanwhile, you have paid the fifteen dollars. It is best to do this by check. Just in case another buyer should challenge your purchase. Besides, by now you are pretty sure of the approximate age of the piece. And, the fact it has a mirror puts it into a new category —a bureau.

> Clue 4—The back exterior of the bureau is rough and dark. The boards are of different widths. This is typical of old pieces made to stand against the wall. The unfinished boards have aged naturally. (A good way to tell if a piece is a reproduction.)

You don't really get excited till you unscrew one of the knobs. They are held in place with handmade wooden screws. These were made before 1830.

> Clue 5—The inside of the drawers is unfinished and appears to be pine. This should make it an American piece. Since you aren't an expert on woods, you'll wait on a cabinet-maker's opinion.

> Clue 6—Saw marks reveal the piece was made with a circular saw. Circular saws weren't widely used in America (especially in the country) until 1830.

Finally the movers arrive and you take the piece to the local furniture stripper (or do it yourself. Or you might decide to merely clean up the existing finish). But, you can't help wondering if the piece is mahogany underneath it all.

At some point, after you have had it stripped, you discover the wood is a beautiful walnut. The inside of the drawers is pine. The cabinet man finds an almost matching wooden knob, repairs the wooded foot and uses filler on the sides.

> Deduction—This is an American country piece, handmade. Dating before 1830. It is technically a "bu-

reau" and the mirror belongs—even though the glass is fairly new.

Had you found it in a shop, restored, the price could have been three hundred dollars and up—depending on the shop and the section of the country. So far you are doing fine paying fifteen dollars for purchase, twenty dollars cabinetry repairs and then a few dollars for refinishing supplies. And, the cost of the six pack. Professional stripping adds twenty dollars or more.

You almost forgot that blue-and-white porcelain box with the red ink pad inside. On your first free day, you take it to the local museum and the curator of Oriental decorative arts. To you it looks like early "country" Ming circa 1600. But for a dollar and fifty cents?

Guess what! The curator pronounces it early blue-and-white porcelain of the Ming period. Not the fine porcelain, but who cares? It's Ming, isn't it?

For under a hundred dollars you have acquired an early Empire bureau in solid walnut and an authenticated Chinese Ming box. To make you feel even better, you recall reproductions of the box currently going for eighty dollars in the local shops. Don't feel too smug. There are other days when you will be "had."

Case History 2

A friend calls and tells you her employer, a television spot producer, is going to sell his hundreds of antique props and collectibles. If you hurry down, you'll have first choice. She warns you that the prices won't be cheap. But, there are some unusual pieces.

Inside the studio you find everything from footed French bathtubs to American Indian artifacts. And the prices aren't cheap. The TV producer doesn't have too much knowledge about what he bought—only that the objects interested him at the time. And, could be used for photo props in his commercials. You pass up the old doorknobs, chandeliers, and shelves of miscellany. It appears you will pass completely this round. Then, your hunter's instinct is aroused at the sight of two glass decanters. They sparkle back at you—for fifteen dollars apiece. Running your finger over their raised design you notice it isn't sharp. That rules out cut glass. Yet, the pattern is a combination of popular cut-glass designs. To further confound you, the bottom has a rough pontil mark. Looking at the plain surfaces you search for a signature or manufacturer's mark. There is none. Still the pieces are handsome, so you purchase them both.

Facts—Decanter has a pattern; a rough pontil mark. The piece has no ring when tapped. The pattern is dull to the touch. There is a mold seam.

Deduction—This is late pressed glass—probably known by various trade names as Nu-cut or Pres-cut. It was an inexpensive way to create the effect of cut glass. It may date from the 1890s to 1906.

Case History 3

On a rainy Saturday morning, you persuade your husband to join you housesaling. Your first stop is in an apartment in a close-in suburb. The ad said, "antiques and miscellaneous to close out estate." A "for rent" sign on the entrance door tells you this is a four-room apartment. Hopefully, every room crammed with antiques. Imagine your surprise when the door is answered by an old acquaintance from your college days. Since he only collects old uniforms and swords, he isn't interested in his aunt's effects.

Happily you find a patchwork quilt for twenty-five dollars, two blown-glass plates for a dollar each and a tall chest of drawers painted glossy black. The chest of drawers puzzles you. By now your husband thinks you've spent enough money and hopes you aren't considering the chest of drawers. But what a challenge! Even through the black paint you make out the outline of the hardware—the Chippendale Willow design. Opening a drawer you come across clue one.

Clue 1—Hand-dovetailed drawers front and back. The piece has rough pine lining the drawers. And, peering into the vacant drawer slot, you can see a couple of knotholes, in rough finish. The piece at that point appears to be before 1840.

Clue 2—The ball feet have a turnip shape. They are mounted on wooden casters. This type of foot can be of Pennsylvania or New York State origin, and might make the piece around 1800. The wooden casters are also a good sign of early nineteenth century.

Discrepancy—Paneling on the back used in late Victorian period.

Your husband helps you out with the piece, growling, drawer by drawer. The first thing you do when you get the piece home is remove the drawer pull. Lucky you, the paint washes off with the help of an S.O.S. pad. It looks like old brass. You grab a magnet, and test the pull. No such luck. It is only plated brass, over iron or steel. The magnet clings. There goes the Chippendale-era theory.

117

You reason that possibly you can use a little elbow grease and more S.O.S. pads to remove some of the paint on the chest. This will save you a "stripper" bill or remover costs.

Sure enough the paint washes away and guess what emerges? A beautiful tiger maple. You do the same for one of the feet. It is curly maple. Where the hardware was removed you see the circular mark of the original knob.

> Deduction—Putting the tiger maple, hand-dovetailing and ball or turnip feet together and the paneling, you decide the piece is from the East (circa early 1800s).

The two plates are too large to be cup saucers (5½ inches in diameter). Both seem to be blown in a swirled rib pattern. Each has twenty-four swirls and a narrow rim. Because they have many imperfections it is possible they were throw-aways. Or, they might be contemporary Mexican glass.

> Deduction—Uncertain. Requires further checking. Could be either early American, circa 1810—or Mexican.

Hunter's Tip: Don't pass up a piece of glass because you think it is new and Mexican. Instead, familiarize yourself with the colors and weight of Mexican glass— which is at hand. Work backward with this known quantity and its characteristics. Many early pieces can be passed by because neither seller nor buyer knows the feel and look of really old American glassware.

Sometimes you must make some snap judgments in order to come out ahead. Other times it is necessary to return several times to the same sale. Intuition often tells you there is more than meets the eye. Much digging may be needed to ferret out what you dream is waiting under the coal bin. It is unfortunate, but hunters do tend to fantasize. This is as bad as getting narcosis when deep-sea diving. You ascribe details to objects and places that don't exist. Often you make several foolish buys. Because you want it to be a country pine bed it becomes a country pine bed. In reality, it is a cleverly refinished machine-made maple bed.

Then there's the day when you go to dozens of sales and find nothing. You don't think it's possible to find any good antiques or collectibles anymore. On your way home you zoom past a ramshackle frame house with a "sale" sign in front. But, good old hunter's instinct drags you back. You have picked up a scent. Inside the place you realize no one has changed the kitty-litter box for fifty years. However, a friendly young couple conducting the sale mention they have lived here five years. They hate to leave it—such a charming old home, but circumstances have forced them to sell. Their new apartment won't accommodate the many antiques. The seller tells you a fascinating retired couple lived there. The house had been built in 1870. And, oh yes, there were lots of fruit jars because the owner had canned.

Sure enough there are hundreds of fruit jars and dozens of buyers grabbing them up. There are also many mildewed boxes and books. Three dim bulbs light the entire basement. You can barely make out the outline of a cupboard, towering in the corner. Closer inspection reveals the cupboard section has missing glass. Both top and bottom are painted in an icky green. There are no instant clues as to hardware. However, by running your hand inside and across the back you feel vertical boards. This can mean a country piece made in the 1870s. After all, it was once a farmhouse! No earth-

119

shaking deduction that was. The bottom part of the cabinet is a puzzler. It has one wide door with two carved pillars—one on each side. Accidentally, you find the top and bottom aren't attached. However, there is no price tag. You decide to pass for the moment. Turning to go upstairs you stub your toe on something —a wooden bowl. Instead of kicking it aside you pick it up. Even covered with filth you can discern it is crudely made. Your fingertips trace circular ridges and a slight hump on the bottom. Forgetting all else you dash upstairs to daylight. Though it seems improbable—you have literally stumbled on an early woodenware bowl. Trying to appear casual, you ask the price.

"Oh, I almost forgot about that," smiles the seller. "You can have it for seventy-five cents. We bought it at a New York State auction about ten years ago. I just liked the shape of it."

You, too. That bowl today would go for two hundred dollars at a New York State auction.

A little lemon oil cleans up the bowl beautifully. That should content the average hunter. Not you. Somehow you have the feeling there is one more treasure hidden behind a bag of old magazines. Back you go. This time you take a piece of heavy sandpaper and a flashlight.

The seller greets you like an old friend and becomes very confidential. You learn she is keeping the golden oak and the Empire chests. She had them priced from a hundred and fifty to three hundred dollars and for some reason nobody bought them. It also turns out she isn't much of a housekeeper. Who would ever guess? In fact, most of the things are exactly as they were when she and her husband bought the place years ago. Many of the previous owner's belongings are where they were.

"We remodeled the bathroom, though. Put in a nice formica vanity."

You inquire what happened to the old washbasin and what it might have looked like.

"Gee, it's around here somewhere," she says.

Dashing down to the basement once again you can't seem to find anything remotely like a marble or whatever washbasin or stand. And, the green cupboard is gone. Back upstairs again you find the cupboard with a twenty-five-dollar price tag. Sanding a corner of the top piece you uncover a pine surface. Doing the same with the base section you discover walnut. Still you aren't sure you want to go through lugging, stripping, and refinishing this unknown piece. Meanwhile, back you go to the kitchen. Opening doors, poking behind the sink you discover—the missing washbasin. It is 12 inches in diameter with a delicate dark-blue pattern on its white porcelain bowl. A find for four dollars and perfect for the small powder room. In a generous moment, the seller lowers the price of the cupboard to twenty dollars. Her husband loads it into the station wagon.

Later when you have had a chance to use some stripper on the cupboard and examine it more carefully, you decide the top was a hanging wall cupboard. It was made in the middle Victorian period. A nice country piece for ten dollars. The base has definite Empire styling. But being a country piece, it was probably made much later.

Hunter's Tip: Don't wait too long if you have a suspicion more discoveries can be made. Other hunters may come to the same conclusion. Sometimes you can't make a clean-cut deduction. Not all of the clues may fit together. But, if the price is low enough—and you can always use the object functionally—buy it. It may take a long time to make an accurate deduction as to the age and origin.

Anne Gilbert

If it takes appraisers months or even longer to track down some antiques, why should you expect to do it instantly?

Hunter's Tip: It's to your benefit to find an object that isn't easily identifiable. First, if you don't know what it is, the dealers won't either—and they'll pass it by. Secondly, it may be a one-of-a-kind rarity. So, keep researching.

Here is a real what-is-it to try the soul of any antique hunter. Is it a treasure—or merely a second-hand table somebody botched up by putting on hand-painted and crude art work? And—is the checkerboard top a recent decal? The table was found on the last day of a private housesale held by the owner. She had been a collector, and was moving now to smaller quarters. The table, she claimed, had been in the family for a couple of generations—and they had another one without the "art work" on it. Beyond that she knew nothing of its history. She was asking eighty-five dollars for it because it was in pretty good condition and had wood-inlay banding (a narrow line of veneer running round the cabinet and up and down the legs).

Clues: It was glass on four sides and the top lifted up. The top also was of glass. Inside, the bottom was lined with old wine-colored velvet. The piece was originally a curio cabinet.

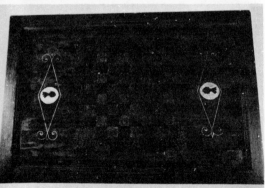

The corners of the cabinet were joined with a handmade mortise and tenons. The bottom, outside, is rough, dark, unfinished, filled with wormholes, and warped.

The slim, tapering leg ending in a spade foot is of Hepplewhite design (1785–1800). The small holes in the inside of the leg mark the missing stretchers. The banding of satinwood was also used by Hepplewhite.

The reversed painting, and the silhouettes painted on the outside, were done by an amateur.

Fact: In the United States reversed painting became popular during the eighteenth and nineteenth centuries. It was a hobby for families to enjoy. An 1857 *Godey's* magazine had a "do-it-yourself" article on how to paint on glass. The silhouettes were to be done with India ink.

Clues: The silhouettes are done with India ink. The glass itself looks to be middle-nineteenth century—certainly not early nineteenth.

The lock should offer clues to the hunter who researches in that category. The lock in this instance is newer than the cabinet.

Deductions: The piece itself is of the Hepplewhite period. The silhouettes and reversed painting were done later, from the 1840s to 1860. Since the piece is a rarity—a one-of-a-kind—it has a value more than the eighty-five dollars paid for it.

Without a doubt, most of the best Shaker furniture resides in museums and private collections. But, since you don't live in a museum one or two pieces should be enough for you. The trick is to find it—and recognize it. Many times a simple Shaker chair may be passed up because it looks (to the untrained eye) like an Appalachian piece made yesterday. Amazingly, there are some early Shaker pieces stashed away in attics. They come to light dusty and in sad shape at garage and similar sales. Because they aren't recognized by the seller you may find one for as little as four dollars—or as much as twenty dollars. If I can do it, so can you.

First, realize there were Shaker colonies in Kentucky, Ohio, and Indiana, as well as the Eastern states. Remember—furniture traveled with people to new settlements outside the colonies. Thus Shaker may turn up thousands of miles from its origins. If you don't feel confident about your finds, refer to them as "Shaker type" until you discover otherwise.

A Shaker "type" chair, positively identified.

Facts: The earliest Shaker chairs were made with splint seats, before 1830. Material was stuffed between the top and bottom of the seats. After 1850, Shaker chairmakers of New Lebanon, New York, mass-produced chairs and

rockers, but not with splint. Woven-cloth tape and cane were used. The Shakers, wishing to combine design form with practicality, used parallel "score" lines to mark location of slats and rungs. The knobs or "finials" on the chair back post can show what colony the chair came from. Shapes may vary from flame to acorn, or round with a small topknot.

Clue: The chair viewed overall shows the Shaker characteristics. There is a missing back stretcher (rung). In the enlarged section, the hand-carved stretcher and worn top of leg post are visible. Score lines and splint seat show up.

Deduction: It is a Shaker "type"—possibly from a colony in the Midwest. Research into designs of the colonies will bring the proper colony to light.

Refinished bureau becomes a chest without the mirror. Under the dark mahogany stain was a beautifully grained walnut wood. The overhang of the top drawer is a clue to its design period—Empire.

Handcarved dovetails at both front and back of drawers is proof of its early origins.

The acanthus leaf carved trim was typical of early American Empire decorations. These could be purchased by cabinetmakers, along with other types of designs and moldings, and applied by them.

The canted bracket feet and scalloped apron front are holdovers from popular early-nineteenth-century country styles.

Clue: Wide wooden knobs have hand-turned wooden screws. Back is rough, unfinished and darkened.

Here's a toughie to figure out. As you can see it was originally painted dark black, including the hardware. Stripping off one side, I discovered the original knobs or pulls had been round (the imprint was there). The wood is a handsome tiger maple. Drawers are doubly dovetailed. Inside drawers are pine. Fluting carved into sides. Feet are Pennsylvania or Eastern type, solid tiger maple, on wooden casters. It appears to be a mid-Victorian piece—possibly made in the East.

Is it just a salad bowl from the dime store (top) or can it possibly be early American woodenware?

Clue: Uneven circumference and rough exterior finish. Burl on bottom of bowl. Handcarved edge. Lathe turned.

Facts: Burl bowls were made by American Indians, totally by hand. American colonists made their bowls on a lathe and hollowed out the wood as it was rotated. Sometimes they used hand tools for a beveled edge. This is probably an early-nineteenth-century chopping bowl.

What strange gismo is this with a wooden handle and metal cutting edge? I was lucky to find this in my grandmother's basement and was told it was a cabbage or vegetable chopper.

Would you know the age of this glass decanter by just looking at it? A touch of your fingers would tell you it is pressed glass. A second glance would show it to be pattern molded. The handle is applied. The pattern sparkles brilliantly.

Deduction: Pattern molded probably made around the turn of the century.

This appears to be an old hobnail cologne bottle. But is it?

Facts: Hobnail reproductions have been made for many years. It was a popular post-Civil War pattern. New hobnail "hobs" will be wider spaced. They aren't as heavy as older pieces. The hobs will be in near perfect condition. Or, if the piece is a deliberate attempt to fool, it may have a hob made of glue—to look like a damaged hob—to lure the buyer into thinking this is a clue to age. Use a magnifying glass to gauge if it is glue, or a chipped authentic hob.

Clues: Hobs are fairly close together. The piece is heavy. The pontil is rounded.

Deduction: This isn't a brand-new reproduction. Probably dates early 1900s. It is the thousand-eye pattern, so called because each hob reflects itself many times.

Victorian blue-and-white washbasin. Can easily be adapted to small powder room. Quite a find for a few dollars.

9
Pigeons Flocking to the Flea Market

Sometimes you can have too much of a good thing—like flea markets. The novelty is wearing thin—at least for me. The good old "iffy" flea market has become just another multimillion-dollar big business.

Major cities advertise giant flea markets with "hundreds of sellers under one roof," from coast to coast. Books tell you how to run your own flea market. There is even a flea-market publication and guides to markets all over the United States and Europe. Sure it's handy for both buyer and seller, but doesn't it strike you as just a little too well organized?

Remember the good old days when you never knew

who or what would turn up at the local flea market? Or, for that matter, when the next flea market would be? Now you see the same dealers every week and the same merchandise. And, why not, when the dealers dash to the nearest wholesale gift-shop outlet and buy up the latest European and Asian reproductions. Thus you can find an entire set of *ersatz* early handpainted plates from East Germany—with *Bavarian* stamped on the bottom. The seller has obviously bought up hundreds of decals marked with whatever piques his fancy from Steuben to R. S. Prussia. All he needs to make back his entry fee of a dollar and a half to seven dollars are a few pigeons.

Nothing wrong with that, except when they know what they are selling isn't what they insist it is. But, ho, ho! That's just flea-market gamesmanship! Boys will be boys and dealers will be dealers is the laissez-faire attitude among most browsers. Sure, but never spend more than five dollars on a flea-market item purporting to be an authentic antique. In the first place, if the object is being pushed as authentic Wedgwood or Meissen for twenty-five dollars, when you know it is worth many times more—be suspicious. That sweet old lady must know something you don't know. Why sell something for pennies you can sell for dollars? She isn't doing it out of the goodness of her heart. Inside that panel truck are probably twenty more of each. Or they are back in her yard, aging in the ground.

The best way to buy at a flea market is not ever to ask questions about what looks old. If you don't know the clues the scream "Bennington" at you, you shouldn't be wandering around unattended. The only way you can still find something of value at low flea-market prices is to be patient and thorough in examining things. What's the rush anyhow to dash on to another booth?

My husband is a case in point. He dashes madly from booth to booth and comes to a sliding stop from time to time. He has discovered an antique auto horn, a rare German stein, or a handpainted porcelain pipe bowl. Calling my name at the top of his lungs he is already reaching for his wallet. His eyes are riveted on the object before him. Not on the open box or truck behind the seller, where a box of rubber-and-brass auto horns or pipe bowls or steins are in plain view. That's how sure the seller is of his pigeons. He knows the victim will be too intent on his purchase to even notice there are dozens of other similar objects in the boxes. And, he has every right to be confident. Does my husband bother to use a magnifying glass on the brass section of the auto horn? If so, he would see "Made in Pakistan" stamped into the brass. Does he turn over the beer stein to see if it says "Made in Japan"? Or, does he closely examine the pipe bowl to see if it is handpainted? Usually I manage to save him from anything serious. But, what about the other husbands and wives?

Flea markets seem to bring out the worst in sellers—amateur or professional. Watching them in operation is like standing by as a carnival sharpie uses the old shell game on his "pigeon." Should you let the victim be had or step in and save him at the final moment? After several experiences playing superwoman-to-the-rescue I am convinced it is better to let the victim be had—and be happy.

"This is genuine Old Willowware Wedgwood. Only five dollars a plate," said one flea marketeer to an enraptured lady pigeon. Now, most of us, even from three feet away, would realize the "Willowware" had just been bought at the five-and-ten. Not so this interested buyer. She swallowed every word and uttered ecstatically, "I've always wanted a set of Wedgewood." Added up, a dozen of this type would cost at most sixty dollars. Probably twice as much here than a retail-store purchase of the same pieces.

Turning one plate over, I said in a loud voice, "Oh, look! It says 'Made in Japan!' "

The irate seller informed me these were nevertheless antique Wedgwood—made in Japan. Now there is a misnomer if I ever heard one. To prove his point he began thumbing through a copy of the Warman antique price guide. Then he began flipping through the Kovel price guide, shouting all the while that Japanese Wedgwood was old and collectible. The lady pigeon gave me a dirty look for ruining her illusion of a bargain, as she walked away. "These were made in the 1930s," he bellowed. "See here. Who the hell are you to know more than a dealer?"

From inside his paneled truck hopped a spry, elderly woman who screeched like a harpy that I had spoiled their sale and should be run out of the flea market. Very gently I reminded her she had been trying to cheat a buyer. As a crowd began to gather I found myself wondering if anyone had ever been lynched at a flea market.

Somehow I escaped and resolved to be a silent observer at flea markets from that moment on.

Bottles and insulators are very big at flea markets. The prices are even bigger. Plain, unmarked bottles from the 1900s are priced from five dollars and up. Many are sold, along with handmade candles, by a growing group of the restless younger generation. Flea-market hopping in their campers is a good way for them to see the country without worrying about credit cards or lodging. Most of them begin their journeys digging in ghost towns or city dumps. Their results are referred to as "antique relics." Along with the dirt-encrusted bottles and insulators, they have rusty tin cups and cookware. The bottles and "relics" are a bit more expensive than the older seller's prices. Probably the dirt adds to the salability.

My all-time find at a flea market happened on a hot July day, a year ago. This particular market was newly opened in a drive-in movie theater lot. There were only about fifteen sellers. At first glance, it looked like a lost cause for antique hunting. Some of the "hotter" items were box-lots of gym shoes and fluorescent pink-and-green shirts. Then, zowie! Right under my nose appeared a Christmas tree ornament in the shape of a spaniel. He looked like the Staffordshire dogs pampered by Victorian ladies. And, he was only ten cents. His gold, gilt, and pink ribbon colors were in very good condition considering his age.

"If you like it, I'll sell you the entire bag for a dollar," urged the seller. "We just cleaned the attic at my mom's and you wouldn't believe the junk."

It was truly Christmas in July. I was almost afraid to open the brown bag bulging with Christmas ornaments. Thrusting a dollar into the seller's hand I ripped open the bag. Out tumbled at least ten handblown German ornaments. Among them was a pink slipper with a tiny mouse inside; a clown and two more spaniels were among the beautifully aging ornaments. They could have been made from the 1870s to 1900. When you consider the spaniel alone would cost twenty-five dollars, even if I could find one, this was indeed a bag of treasures.

One good discovery doesn't necessarily make two. Feeling overly confident at flea markets is a big mistake.

For several weeks I picked up what I believed were antique demitasse cups. They had the scroll handle and shape popular in the nineteenth century. Even better, I thought, they had no mark on the bottom. This might mean they were even older. Now if I hadn't been carried away by my own conceit I would have realized by just lifting the cups, they were too heavy to be *that* old. Since then I have learned many are now being made in Japan and Europe. With the label taken off, who knows? I didn't know. But then, I only paid a dollar or two to learn a valuable lesson.

Just for fun, a friend and I decided to set up a booth at the largest drive-in movie flea-market lot in our area. Three dollars purchased our space. We learned the old-timers arrived when the gates opened around seven thirty in the morning. Very good thinking behind this. Tables, blankets, etc. are completely set up before the pigeons begin flying in. Even more to the point, there is additional time for sellers to wheel and deal among themselves before the buyers arrive. Quickly the old-timers converged on our space. Somehow the word had spread that we were strictly one-shot sellers. Hopefully we had some goodies way underpriced that they could resell at a profit. We were practically sold out by nine that morning. Later, we wandered around to see how much of a mark-up had been added to our pieces. One of the most amazing was an amber-and-red glass, nested-chicken dish. My friend had bought it at a gift shop in Vermont for around seven dollars, brand new. We even told the dealer who bought it that it wasn't an old chicken dish. We couldn't convince her. "We've been in business a long time, honey," said the chicken-dish buyer. "We know when a thing is old." We saw it later being resold with a sixty-five-dollar price tag and marked "antique." I wonder if there were any pigeons who purchased it?

We also learned what a temptation it is to try and pass off new pieces as antiques. Invariably every other pigeon asked us, "Is it old?" Somehow it is easier to ask a seller whether a piece is antique than to carefully examine that same object for themselves. Or, to have faith in their own observations. Even stranger were the number of "experts" who pointed out with certainty why a bottle or dish wasn't really antique, when we insisted it wasn't really old. The more we insisted, the more determined the "experts" were it was antique. Perhaps we unknowingly discovered some reverse selling psychology.

Heavy pieces of furniture can be good buys. After all, who wants to lug a chest or heavy chair back and forth? A genuine old Morris chair for fifteen dollars and early Victorian chest of drawers for four dollars were true flea-market values. My friend bought the chest, covered with chipping white paint. When she got the piece home and stripped off the paint, she discovered beautiful birdseye maple. This is why it pays to travel with a station wagon or rent a U-Haul trailer.

If much of this sounds like "sour grapes," remember, better a live skeptic than a shot-down pigeon.

You can be just as much a pigeon on Portobello Road in England as in Oshkosh, Wisconsin. Maybe more so.

As one well-traveled antique dealer told me in a rare moment of truth, "Americans will buy anything in England that looks like Queen Anne furniture or Georgian silver." Consider that the English have been in the antique business a couple of centuries longer than we have. They have also been reproducing antiques longer. So, should you happen to be visiting a British or French flea market—be wary. Look for objects that aren't as popular as Georgian silver. Perhaps some architectural fragments or antique holy-water fonts. Sometimes an Art Deco or art nouveau item. By now these are probably being mass-produced somewhere and put out to pasture at a flea market or two in Europe. Obviously, there are flea markets everywhere in the world. The best advice I can give you is to ask where they are, wherever you travel. The obvious ones are Portobello Road Market in London and the Paris Champs Elysées Flea Market. But there is also the Petticoat Lane Market and Bermondsey Market in London; and the Porte de Clignancourt, Porte de Vanves, Porte de Montreuil, and Place d'Aligre to explore in Paris. You'll find flea markets in the provincial towns of France. When you consider that the French started the whole flea-market concept in the middle of the nineteenth century, no wonder there are so many markets. The original in Paris, the Porte de Clignancourt is not only still standing, but considered one of the outstanding flea markets of the world (if a flea market can be outstanding). There are today over two thousand sellers. There are markets in Germany, Italy, Greece, Holland, Portugal, Switzerland, Spain—in short, everywhere. If you don't speak any foreign language, consider hiring a student to go with you, from a local school. Then, apply the same hunter's technique you do at home—with your friend doing the bargaining. Just remember to steer clear of items you see by the dozen. Use that magnifying glass.

Because flea markets are such big business in the United States, they are no longer seasonal. You'll find them being run twice a month at county fairgrounds around the country—often in heated exhibition buildings. Community houses often run flea markets once a month. Many are sponsored by charitable organizations.

I must admit, the sellers, be they dealers or amateurs, get my sympathy. They put in long hours of what must be a bit of a bore. Usually to earn fifty dollars or less.

Where does all the money go? To the man at the top, the flea-market manager. While the sellers are sweating or freezing, the owner of the chain of flea markets can go sailing on his yacht—or whatever pleases his fancy. Who needs him till it's time to count the money? Multiply the three to seven dollar a head of sellers by one hundred. Then, add to that a crowd of from five hundred to five thousand at fifty cents a head. Do some more adding, if the same person owns more than one location. It almost beats owning parking lots. So, now, who are the biggest pigeons? Buyers or sellers? Who cares? Where else can you take the whole family for such cheap entertainment?

An unusual Victorian Christmas ornament found at a July flea market in a bag with many other ornaments. Combines cardboard Santa and child figure with wire and handblown glass.

More flea market Christmas ornament discoveries. On the left, a plaster angel, and on the right a devil's head in glistening red.

Sometimes you can find bargains at the flea market. A bag of old Victorian Christmas ornaments for a dollar or two has to be a treasure. Here are some found on one July day. These quaint shapes were probably done by one family. Fathers and sons would blow them and the women would paint them. This cottage industry had no competitors til their export stopped during World War I. These ornaments, shop priced, would be from five dollars to twenty-five dollars each.

THEY ARE MIGHTY SWELL IN

THEY ARE ALL GOOD LOOKERS IN

Shades of Rudolph Valentino! These highly collectible postcards were sent in a series from a "fellow to his girl." They were found for a dime for a set of four at a flea market. Postcard freaks would doubtless be willing to pay quite a bit more—they are unusual. If you care to spend the time pawing over hundreds of boxes of postcards, doubtless you'll find some unusual additions for your collection.

Cups and saucers of all descriptions turn up on flea-market tables. It is up to you to know which are authentic Victorian demitasse or mugs. Dainty light-weight porcelain "singles" with no marking can be yours for a dollar or two. The early Victorian demitasse cups and saucers weren't always marked. Left, an early Victorian find. Sometimes a copper-luster mug (right), will be mistaken for a contemporary mug because of its almost gaudy colors and bold designs. One dollar at a flea-market booth. It dates to the 1830s with its raised floral motif. The small indentation on the lip was a rest for the spoon.

Old stoves and heaters of every description pop up at flea markets. If you have a sturdy arm and lots of rust remover you can probably find a charmer for three dollars. Country shops are no place to search for bargain prices. This is best found at flea markets.

There are always lots of nested glass animal and fowl dishes at flea markets. The trick is to recognize the authentic oldie. It is getting harder to do with supermarkets offering new colorful glass versions and fancy gift shops selling similar "Made in Portugal" versions. Most often reproduced are the milk glass. Held to light, they should have a slightly opalescent look (left). Bargain from a Paris flea market is this signed milk glass Vallerystahl chicken dish (right). An authentic camphor glass chicken, found at antique shop sale for less than value. Many camphor reproductions are similar but heavier and without the grayish look of the old pieces.

Small glass antiques can be picked up for under a dollar—if you look sharp at flea markets. This candy measure was found for a quarter (left). The syrup pitcher, or individual creamer, was found for seventy-five cents at a flea market. Similar ones have turned up at basement sales. Candy measure is about one inch high. Pitcher is two inches.

Glass salt dips are easy to find at flea markets. But even some of these have been reproduced. Be sure you take a good look before you buy.

10
Should You Bring Home a Wounded Antique?

EVERY SO OFTEN hunters find it hard to resist bringing home a wounded antique—especially if said piece is an uncommon one at an El Cheapo price. The dealer who sells you that early pressed-glass candy dish with the crack across the bottom is all heart. He will sacrifice this old rarity for twenty-five dollars. Heaven only knows when you'll see this scarce pattern again. He tries to convince you the crack doesn't really mean anything with so scarce an antique. There are collectors who would offer him more just to add it to their collection. The same piece in mint condition would command twice as much, he insists. Besides, perhaps an

Anne Gilbert

expert glass repairman can "do something to make sure the crack doesn't grow." Wondrous things are being done these days in the field of antique restorations. Would a museum pass up such a piece just because of a crack? What should you do?

You can be philosophical about it and buy. But in this instance you would be smarter to leave it with the dealer who loves it, and will care for it. Now, if that same piece is offered to you at a rummage sale for a couple of dollars, buy it. The piece is still serviceable and as long as you keep it filled with candy nobody will notice its scars.

The smartest hunters I know don't buy wounded antiques from dealers. They *do* buy them at house and garage sales. A friend of mine makes a nice profit re-selling wounded porcelain antiques she has repaired with one of the new "china repair kits." Or, some she keeps to fill out collections. A perfect example was a vegetable dish in the old moss-rose pattern purchased for a quarter at a housesale. One handle was broken off the side, and lying in the dish. The top had been poorly mended with an old-fashioned glue that had yellowed with age. My talented friend literally took the whole thing apart and skillfully put it back together. She sold it for five dollars at her next garage sale—to a dealer.

It isn't every day you run across a handsome nine-teenth-century mantel clock for forty dollars, complete with original papers identifying the maker. There is only one small thing wrong—it has no pendulum and, of course, isn't working. Before you buy you have two things to consider.

1. What would it cost to repair?
2. What is its current market value in working condition?

There is, of course, a third consideration: Either you know how to fix it yourself or you have a friend who can find parts and loves to put clocks together for friends.

If the clock is outwardly in mint condition, and you know it will be a long time before you find an authentic mantel clock by this name clockmaker, grab it. Don't be in a hurry to farm it out for repairs. Shop around for a reputable clock repairman. Check through your museum to find who they use to make and repair old parts. If you are not concerned with reselling the clock to a collector the repairs won't matter. New parts do lower the value for dedicated clock collectors. But what do you care, if that friendly "bong" is what you crave?

Some of your best buys in wounded antiques may very well be in furniture. In the first place you'll have less competition from professional dealers when shopping at housesales. They have to figure their time to either do the repairs themselves or the cost to farm it out. Usually they'll pass by chairs that need recaning or reupholstering. A broken leg or arm, a missing spindle or stretcher get thumbs down from them. Should you buy? Here again you have to weigh the facts. How much do you want that Victorian rocker with the missing cane seat? What will it be worth in mint condition versus the cost for repairs?

Buy:

If you like to strip, reupholster and refinish yourself.
If it is priced from 50 cents to ten dollars.
If it is handcrafted or early nineteenth century or earlier piece.

Are you willing to turn your garage or basement into a workroom, and suffer the fumes of paint and varnish remover? Do you have the patience to buy a caning kit and do the job yourself? If there are missing knobs, handles, or panes of glass are you willing to patiently search for the proper period hardware or be satisfied with reproduction hardware? The reproduced hardware can be found advertised in such antique publications as *Hobbies* magazine, *Collector's News* and *Collector's Weekly.*

For some time now I have had a leaded-glass church window gathering mildew in my garage. It has a missing pane and another with a crack. It was one of those impulse things—the winning five-dollar bid at a country auction. I should have probably let it pass. But the thought of a leaded-glass window for five dollars was too good to pass by. I didn't stop to think about the cost of repairs. Is there a repair specialist close by? What would he charge? The cheapest estimate I have come up with after trying all over my area is seventy-five dollars, which would bring my antique leaded window cost to eighty dollars, plus installation costs. Perhaps this is a reasonable price. But, I'm still shopping around. I've also toyed with the idea of mailing away for a leaded-glass window repair kit with decorations. In the meantime, I keep wondering where it was I had planned to put the blasted window in the first place.

To my way of thinking the better buys in antique furniture are upholstered pieces oozing their innards. Sometimes a simple touch of a hammer and the addition of a couple of carpet tacks and tape will suffice. I have a fond memory of an upholstered Eastlake Victorian side chair. The back and seat were covered in a delicate rosebud print, in good condition. This seemed to be the original fabric. At first glance any potential buyer could see the bottom was falling apart and the same for the chairback. The chair was reduced at this housesale to twelve dollars. During these closing hours it was almost the only thing left. As any antique hunter knows a similar chair in good condition would certainly get at least fifty dollars. Naturally I brought it home and applied first aid—a couple of carpet tacks and tape. The stuffing almost complete. Presto, it looked to be in pretty good shape. It sold at a friend's garage sale for twenty-five dollars. I would have kept it—except I'm running out of room. You might say this is one of the chronic diseases of the hunter—not knowing when to stop bringing things home.

Now, if the chair had required major surgery it could have been more than the value. If you can do a creditable upholstery job then such a chair would be a good buy. One friend has taken advantage of the current patchwork craze. Instead of spending money on upholstery fabric for a love seat, she has created her own patchwork fabric. The loveseat originally cost her five dollars in tacky condition at a garage sale. She stripped off the finish and took it apart. However, she is a patient soul who just restores in her spare time.

A dealer-collector acquaintance has a thing for old radios. His apartment is filled with a fantastic array of radios and radio parts. He can pick up a "case" that strikes his fancy at one housesale, and old radio tubes at flea markets. Yes, if you've always wondered who buys old radio tubes, that's who.

Old picture frames—especially the gilded plaster variety—cost a fortune in perfect condition. In the good old days I used to find them with missing pieces priced for a couple of dollars. No more. Even with missing leaves and scrollwork, people snap them up. They know they can repair them with chewing gum, molded into the correct design, then sprayed with gilt. Or, there are kits for fussy do-it-yourselfers. This enables you to pick up a 3 x 4 foot frame for five dollars, and repair it for a couple more. The value of course makes this a worthwhile project.

If you aren't handy there is the danger of just accumulating a lot of potential firewood furniture.

If a piece needs major repairs think twice—unless you can make your own furniture parts in your workshop. One fortunate couple works as a team restoring and refinishing antiques. They buy from dealers, and pay a hefty price in the first place for an old pine cabinet or schoolmaster's desk in need of repairs. They have figured out that for them the price isn't too high if the piece is rare enough. They have made a study of the design elements of the period they collect. So, when the husband makes a wooden knob, or drawer, it is true to the original design, wood, and finish. Refinishing is his wife's specialty. She has even studied up on the old methods of color dye, and staining for total authenticity. That's a real purist. Unfortunately not everyone has the time, dedication, or talent.

Word of mouth is one of the best ways to find outstanding repair craftsmen. Yes, there are times when only the best will do. You must make up your mind to get a bank loan to pay for restoration.

You might begin by asking around in the antique departments of quality stores. Hopefully they'll tell you where they go for repairs. Do the same at quality antique galleries. Of course, they may not tell you—if repairs are among their services. Keep trying. Sooner or later you will find out how to eliminate this "middleman" expense.

Your next step is to check with friends who have had antiques well-repaired. After that it's between you and the yellow pages of the phone book. However, select the advertiser who mentions "being in business twenty years or more." Or "second-generation cabinetmakers." Visit their shops. As true artisans they will welcome a chance to show you their work—and take pride in explaining how they do it. Treat them gently. Often they are quite elderly and temperamental. If they don't like your attitude, as far as they are concerned, you can go elsewhere. They also will probably inform you that it will be months before they can finish your repairs, and perhaps you should go elsewhere. You will have found your craftsman at this point. Encourage him by telling how old the object is and how you love the old hand-crafted pieces. He, too, appreciates "your type of antiques," and will actually be quite anxious to work on it.

These old-timers pride themselves on workmanship, whether it's making a set of wooden clockworks or putting a rolltop back in rolling condition. You and they know that there isn't anyone to carry on when they retire. Many have trained relatives to take over. But, alas, not enough. And it is this dedication and craftsmanship that costs you so much money. The dedicated hunter will know it's worth every dollar to have a fine piece restored. A shoddy job leaves you with a worthless antique.

Advertising-tin collectors always have a tough decision to make when a rare tin is rusty and discolored. While Rust-oleum works wonders on many tins, it isn't a certainty. So, specialists in this field suggest buying damaged tins for pennies. If Rust-oleum, washing with a gentle liquid soap, and waxing doesn't do it, at least it was cheap. In this case, save it as a "rare display piece." Next time you see one you'll recognize it instantly. Whatever you do, don't throw it out. The same might be said for advertising trade cards. Better to have some cheap examples till something better comes along

—at your price. Most damage comes to trade cards that have been pasted in scrapbooks by original owners. Trying to remove them can be a tricky proposition. To soak or not to soak—that is the question.

There is a happier note to buying other paper antiques such as color prints. Many times you can find a rare print, such as an early railroad print, inexpensively. The reason—foxing. Foxing is another term for the brown spots that result from age, dampness, etc. A quick bath in a "bleach and water" solution often removes the stains. It also brightens up the print. This is a good way to tell whether a more expensive print has been recently handcolored—or was done in the nineteenth century. I know it's hard to believe, but many print dealers have discovered they can buy up batches of old black-and-white book plates and have them inexpensively handcolored. They can be then sold at considerable profit. It can be an expensive "lesson" for the duped buyer "testing the color."

A real no-no is the print that has been trimmed to size. This happened with many old Currier and Ives prints . . . and cuts down their value. In the case of other prints this is just as true—and it eliminates the name of the engraver.

What it all comes down to is whether the ultimate value or rarity of the antique is worth the time, trouble, and expense of restoration. Only you can make that decision.

This wounded Victorian washstand with spool legs is missing its towel bar and is in need of refinishing. Should it be passed up for four dollars? Made of pine, and in otherwise good condition, it is a handy night table. I can live without the towel bar for the moment. This type of "find" probably wouldn't satisfy the purist.

Sometimes a wounded antique can be turned into a totally new object—and lead a useful life. This gilded zinc cupid was saved from the junk heap. When found by a friend, one foot was broken. Cost—about fifty cents. A lamp shop added the lamp fixture, set cupid on a handsome wooden base and fixed his foot for twenty dollars. With a "flickering" bulb he presides over a buffet table.

A Boston rocker for fifty cents. Dusty and with a missing spindle, and the back separated from the seat it seemed a dubious find. A local cabinetmaker made a new spindle and put the entire piece together for under twenty dollars. It must have been a lady's or child's rocker as it is only three feet high, and the seat is a foot-and-a-half wide, made of pine. The clue to its worth was the curve of the sleigh seat—even at twenty paces—that said, "Boston rocker."

You'll cry when you realize this lacy "sandwich type" compote has a crack on its bottom. None the less, I was happy to grab it at a housesale for a dollar and fifty cents. Perhaps it can be fixed. Meanwhile I know the feel, ring, and look of this early pressed glass. Filled with fruit, you can't even see the crack.

A Bennington "type" pitcher with a chipped top. Was it worth buying for two dollars? The happy hunter thinks so. It will help him recognize this type of ware the next time he spots it. Meantime, he may find a way to repair it or someone to put it in shape.

These two pieces are part of a cocoa set, or child's tea set, including six cookie plates, five cups and saucers, sugar bowl, and a pot. Since this is an old, mid-nineteenth-century pattern, it was worth three dollars—even with the missing lid on the pot and minus one cup and saucer. Who knows? Someday you may find matching pieces.

There was a time when you could pick up these country Sheraton side chairs for a couple of dollars—in fairly good condition. Unfortunately for the hunter, they are very popular and simple to recognize. This is one of a pair bought for seven dollars for both. They needed stripping and recaning. Unless you know a cheap place that does caning, they may not be worth the expense. Check the craft departments of senior citizen groups and homes for the elderly. Often the senior citizens will welcome something to do—and the cost will be less for a job well done. The other alternative is to write to the mail-order caning suppliers and do-it-yourself cheaply. If you are lucky you'll find a couple of these chairs in a garage or basement for ten dollars each. Where can you buy a new chair for that these days that is sturdy?

11
Hunting Tips for Travelers

ONCE THE ANTIQUE hunter has "bagged" successfully in familiar hunting spots, close to home, the urge to try his or her luck in new areas is overwhelming. Basically, whether you hunt in Honolulu or Hackensack, the rules are pretty much the same.

Hunting spots are like toadstools—they bloom and thrive in some unlikely places. It is the task of the hunter to quickly differentiate between the toadstools and the prize mushrooms without sampling them financially. Sometimes, however, even the most knowledgeable hunter "bites" without thinking. While not fatal, it can be a most unpleasant experience.

Consider the quaint country shop festooned with a

charming wishing well and an old barn, bulging with forgotten treasures for the hunter. Before you start frothing at the mouth consider that you aren't its first discoverer. If it is on a dirt side road, be all the more suspicious. Much thought and planning went into placing it in an out-of-the-way location. Maybe that folksy farm couple don't look like the antique dealers in the city. Caution: if anything, they are better versed on prices and the current fad collectibles.

One of my favorite hunting adventures took me down Wisconsin's main highways and back-country roads. Collectors are forever coming back from Friendship, Wisconsin, or Door County with the most fantastic hunting yarns. Currently half of the hunters from Iowa and Illinois to Michigan and Indiana must be hunting in Wisconsin. There are visions of empty barns waiting to be ransacked. (Remember some hunters have no scruples.) Wisconsin is the current favorite, inasmuch as Iowa, Illinois and the rest of the Midwest are pretty well picked over.

According to my hunting friends, the things to look for in Wisconsin are American primitives. The beloved oak icebox, Indian rugs, and early American pressed glass are hunted down relentlessly. There are flea markets on the weekend and country auctions almost every evening.

Who could pass up such a hunting challenge? Waupaca and Kaukauna look out! We (my husband and I) passed through Chicago and headed to the Interstate 90 and north on Wisconsin 13 to Wisconsin Dells.

We came to a quick stop in front of the picturesque beauty of an old well. It led to a farmhouse and barn offering "antiques."

After knocking on the door for five minutes an elderly woman answered. She let us know immediately that she couldn't see or hear very well. Judging by the number of reproductions in pressed glass and china, obviously she needed new glasses. However, my first reaction was to be dazzled by dozens of shelves, strategically placed in the windows, filled with glassware. Here were all those favorite old patterns, from ribbed-grape to Bellflower. There were also Shirley Temple mugs and Depression glass. In the china section, R. S. Prussia galore. In short, nothing different than in most shops around the country. Strangely enough the prices were higher than in neighboring Chicago. However, I wasn't ready to give up. There were still a shed and barn to plow through. The shed contained the primitives in profusion; the barn, furniture. If I had been smart enough to bring a trailer or station wagon I could have come away with a novel chest and some small display cabinets for less than city prices. Probably because most people don't come equipped with U-Hauls. I ended up spending a dollar for a butter chip in an old pattern for a fellow collector. At home I would have probably paid a quarter. But, this was tourist-hunting season.

I fell in love with Friendship, Wisconsin. Not so much for its antiques as its Friendship Café. Where else could we find a sandwich of homemade bread, filled with thick slices of Wisconsin sausage, and spread with real butter for thirty-five cents?

The Friendship Auction and Antique Store was my next hunting stop. Hunters can't miss its brightly painted door and sign. The same assortment of pressed glass, chamber pots, and country furniture seen at another shop were in abundance. And Shirley Temple appeared again, priced on par with other area shops. This brings us to:

Hunter's Traveling Tip: Find one or two currently popular collectibles or antiques to use as a price gauge in other hunting spots. In other words, a Shirley Temple mug can range from six dollars to twelve dollars from place to place.

In Wisconsin Rapids, we discovered Barrett's Auction barn. At last, a genuine Midwestern country auction! Lucky us! There was to be one that very night.

Fortunately we arrived well before the auction to look around. Many antiques were for sale in the store area. And the prices weren't cheap. Oh well, on with the auction. The auctioneer must have been trained in the city. He was a sharpie, intimating a box of porcelain salt shakers might contain a piece of Nippon or valuable collectibles. Just like home! It was very big on old over-stuffed chairs and used electric fans. What antiques there were sold for more than their dubious value.

Hunter's Traveling Tip: Don't get carried away at country auctions, especially during tourist season.

Somehow after leaving Wisconsin Rapids we took a wrong turn and traveled many miles on a dusty country road. Suddenly, like a mirage in the desert, we came upon a trading post. It had to be a hunter's paradise. Wagon wheels, bottles, and farm equipment were piled in front of the shedlike building. With my heart beating fast I leaped out, hoping the owner was inside. Was he ever! He put down his antique price guide long enough to nod and invite me to "have a look. I've got lots of Depression glass." Apparently he took the price guide to heart and had marked up prices accordingly. My eye fastened on a Mrs. Butterworth's syrup bottle, empty, for two dollars.

Hunter's Tip: Keep your eye out for currently manufactured objects such as Mrs. Butterworth's bottles, Lancer's Rosé stoneware, and Paul Masson heart-shaped sherry bottles. If they are for sale empty for more than you can still buy them for full, be a bit suspicious of the seller.

Farewell to the trading post and on to Door County, famed as an artists' colony and antique collector's heaven. Here antiques and collectibles are sold with a sophisticated eye. The Pine Hill Shop is a lovely private home converted to a thriving antique shop. Here we found primitives and handsome authentic pieces—side by side with reproductions. The prices were high and the place was crammed with customers. In fact, business was so good the owner was complaining about too many people. I weakened and bought an unusual figural bottle of Father Christmas dating before 1900, for thirty dollars. While it's against my better judgment to spend that much for an old bottle, this one seems to be an uncommon one. Hopefully, someday I'll find it cataloged for twice as much. At least its seam lines and peeling painting tell me it isn't a reproduction.

Since I wasn't doing too well with my hunting, I decided to try another tactic:

Hunter's Traveling Tip: Ask in towns where the thrift and resale shops or Salvation Army places are located. In Kewaunee, local residents told me about the resale shop in the old Kewaunee train depot. Sure enough there was used furniture, china, lamps, and even a Civil War razor. At last, a new hunting preserve! For two dollars I picked up a Shaker-style chair, three copper and iron yokes for a dollar fifty and a Victorian plant stand with spool legs for two dollars.

From there on it was all downhill. However, if I had had the time to ask where the local resale shops were, the results might have been more successful.

I have friends who swear Indiana, especially Madison, is great antique-hunting territory. This quaint river town looks for all the world to be untouched by tourism. Still another hunter informs me one of the shop owners brings her pieces from her Chicago shop to Madison and ups the price for summer tourist traffic. American primitives go great here and you can doubtlessly find many chests, beds, and desks dating to the 1800s—priced in the hundreds of dollars. Still, if you like primitives and can afford it—now is the time to buy. Otherwise, haunt the housesales wherever you live.

Hunter's Traveling Tip: Realize that antiques traveled with their owners. You can find them many thousands of miles from their origin.

The state of Illinois, with its major cities, would seem to offer fertile hunting in the country towns and suburbs. One cold spring day another hunter and I, quite by accident, took a wrong turn in a road—adjacent to an Illinois expressway. It seems we always are off the path. We both spotted the same sign, "Happy Acres Antiques," fronting a charming old country farmhouse (aren't they all?). The sign stated hours were from 1:00 P.M. to 4:00 P.M. Our antique gold watches told us we had five minutes before one. Even from the car windows we could see a converted chicken house; windows sparkling with old china and glass. Milk cans by the door. Leaping from the car we peered in those windows like children exclaiming, "Look at this." or "Look at that." Here were goblets in Ruby Thumbprint, Westward Ho, and Three Faces. Naturally we began pounding on the door. No one answered but a dog began barking. Turning toward the house we saw a giant beast snarling through the window.

"You go knock on the door," suggested my friend. Just then the kitchen door opened. Out charged a woman and the dog.

"We wanted to look at your antiques," my friend said, smiling bravely.

Looking us up and down, from head to toe, the woman said, "I don't open till one."

By now it was one, we pointed out.

"What are you interested in?"

Like most hunters we really didn't have anything specific in mind and said so. At that point we should have gotten back into the car. But, here we were, practically begging this woman to allow us to come in and spend our money in her shop. Shrugging indifferently she let us in—chaining the growling dog just outside the door.

Before we knew it my friend had bought several goblets in the Ruby Thumbprint pattern. If she hadn't been so excited over discovering them she would have realized they were reproductions—priced high. I was no smarter. "How old is this glass swan?" I asked.

She gave the standard reply, reserved for dolts. "Very old." By then, my friend had spent fifty dollars on glassware. And, I had spent fifteen on a circa 1927 swan. None of this endeared us to the owner. She snarled throughout the entire transaction and asked for every kind of identification but our gold fillings as we wrote out checks. Not too long after this, I spotted her buying at one of the antique shows. Meaning her mark-up in the country shop was higher than the antique show prices—even with a dealer's discount.

There is an interesting phenomenon that occurs in some country shops. The owners become so attached to their pieces they refuse to part with them. Woe betide the poor hunter who happens upon one of these eccentrics. It also happens in the suburbs. In fact, one located in a Midwestern suburb is especially hard on the unsuspecting hunter. Be advised, however, I found its counterpart in the Berkshires.

The scene opens something like this. The door is heavily padlocked from the inside, or outside. The windows are filled with Victorian goodies and unusual collectibles. Inside there is a dim light shining.

The eager hunter bangs on the door. Finally an elderly lady or man totters to the door. Through the door the dealer asks, "What do you want?" He or she may or may not let you in. Assuming the padlocks are removed, you enter with glazed eyes. Where to look first!

"The owner isn't in, so I don't know if I can sell you anything," is the pitch. What the dealer means is that his other half is probably upstairs or in the back room, waiting for the right psychological moment to enter the shop. All the china, glassware, silver, gold, boxes, etc. are locked up in display cabinets. For the first time you notice the dealer carries a huge key ring (antique, of course) that looks like something a jailer in a dungeon would wear. No matter what you ask for in the cabinets, you are told: "Oh, that is part of my collection." "There isn't a price on that and the owner isn't here." "I don't know if I can sell that."

Finally, if you persevere, the dealer will open a cabinet and take out the little black box inlaid with mother-of-pearl. Peering at it the dealer will say sixteen dollars. Now, if this sounds like an outlandish price you must stand your ground and say, "Are you sure you are reading that price correctly?" This gives the dealer a chance to reconsider and come up with a lower figure and a sale—maybe. The fun comes when you open the package outside the store and see the price is either four dollars or there's no price at all. Or, the dealer may have removed the tag after selling it, which is logical. There are times when hunters may be less fortunate and the other dealer comes swooping into the shop. Well I recall one man who came yelling into the room and practically grabbed my selection out of my hand. "You can't sell that," he bellowed. "Why did you open the shop today, anyhow?" Then looking at me he roared, "We're closed." What should the hunter do? Beg for the purchase at any price or leave? The smart hunter takes off fast. When you've seen this routine once, it's enough.

As if just being in the country isn't enough for country shops, the "country store" antique shop is coming to the towns. They are outfitted to look like the old one-room general stores. They feature old-store cash registers and cutesy decor with penny candy and pickles. There's one in New Market, Tennessee, appropriately named "The Olde Store" that has some very unique claims to fame. It boasts a few of the original store items, left over from its historical past. Among them, a walnut coffin, complete with the skeleton of a woman. In case you pass that way, the owner has let it be known he is searching for other similar old-store items for this section. Besides the coffin he has Victorian furniture, and hundreds of antiques and collectibles. The hardest part for most hunters would be getting past the casket.

Hunter's Traveling Tip: If country stores and their contents are what you seek, make a stop at the main library in each town. Or, the county courthouse department of buildings and records. What you are after is locations of stores and buildings before 1900, or thereabouts. If they are still in existence you may be able to buy old tins or coffee grinders from the current owner. Much cheaper than bidding on them at auctions or paying shop prices.

Sometimes miracles do happen to collectors—almost in their own backyard. Imagine, for instance, coming across three deserted, boarded-up buildings dating from 1870 to 1935, still filled with their original merchandise. Building one is a neighborhood tavern, building two a general store, building three is a three-story department store. Inside, it is as if time had stood still. Only the dust and cobwebs tell you they are from another age. The tavern with its heavy mahogany bar has the same bar glasses and decanters in place behind the bar.

There is even a pipe rack where patrons kept their favorite pipes. The pipes, mostly long-stemmed with porcelain bowls, are still in place—waiting for their owners.

Inside the general store are old tins filled with tea, tobacco, and bolts of cloth, exactly as they were at the turn of the century. There is pressed glass, cut glass, and you-name-it. They are as new as the day they were made. Inside the department store are old-new (or is it new-old?) objects dating up till 1935. Sound incredible? Not really. Bernie Edwards of Northbrook, Illinois, a collector of clocks and advertising tins, discovered such buildings. It nearly unhinged his mind. Here were advertising tins of every description, dolls, glassware, in their original mint condition.

It all began when a caretaker for the buildings called Bernie and told him he had lots of "old stuff" to get rid of as the buildings would soon be demolished. The old man had already given away the iron toys to neighborhood youngsters. The only problem was that the old fellow wanted to make his sales piecemeal—for the sake of his social security. He based his prices on what looked interesting to him. Hence a tobacco or tea tin would be of little value—some beer steins would be correspondingly expensive.

At first glance it would seem that Bernie Edwards would become a millionaire overnight, or over several nights. At the current prices of these items, only the best can happen to him.

On the other hand, look at it this way. Suddenly the antique market is deluged with thousands of once scarce objects. The bottom could fall out of nostalgia for all time. What will finally happen is not certain. It is my guess that Bernie will sell off a few items at a time to keep the value up, and move the three buildings to a vacant lot near his home. Or, he can turn the place into one of those "trading post" museums and let visitors buy at leisure. Who knows, maybe you'll discover a boarded-up glass factory. Anything can happen to a collector!

When is an antique store not an antique store? When it is an antique store masquerading as a museum. One outstanding example is located in a Midwestern resort town. It calls itself a museum, but not only charges admission—it sells its displays. No well-informed hunter would be trapped in one of these. But, if you realize what is going on it's worth a visit. The owner informs the hunter that his admission price can be applied on any purchase. Fair enough? As the hunter wanders through rooms filled with relics, antiques, and collectibles he is informed by the owner that this is a carefully collected history of objects used in this area from the 1800s to 1935. "That's the cut-off date," he reminds you. As your eyes light on that good old empty Mrs. Butterworth's bottle priced at four dollars, and the heart-shaped Masson sherry bottle, empty for nine dollars, you mutter "umhm."

"There's a dealer in New England who can't get these Butterworth bottles," he explains. "She sells them for ten dollars. Can't get them there," he repeated. Sorry, but he wouldn't tell me who—so I could tell you. Yes, indeedy, antiques do travel!

Before I left the "museum" without buying anything, he said reflectively, "You know, I'm sitting on a gold mine here. That's why I don't have price tags on some things. The price goes up from day to day." Thinking about an oak icebox in one of his rooms priced at three hundred and fifty dollars I was inclined to agree. I also put oak iceboxes on my list of items to judge prices on.

Aging things out in the elements is apparently window dressing for the country shops. The more rusty the iron bedsteads, the more decaying the wicker chairs and stoneware crocks on display, the more drawing appeal. It does have a certain psychological effect—the first few times. After that it is strictly "garbage dump circa 1970s."

When you've sampled all the hunting on the "mainland," try the Hawaiian Islands. Not long ago I combined business with hunting pleasure on two of the islands: Oahu and Kauai. Since on Kauai there were no antique shops per se, I asked around if anyone was selling an estate, or if there were any resale shops. One gift-shop owner just happened to have a collection of unframed Japanese woodcuts—Kabuki and others. Also, some old French prints. All were on consignment and priced from eight dollars for the French prints and from sixty dollars to the high hundreds for the Japanese prints. They looked liked originals, not reprints. Since I don't read Japanese, I couldn't tell who the artists were. Who knows what I may have passed up—a Hokusai or Utamaro. I'll never know. But, if you collected or had researched Japanese prints you would know and perhaps have found a bargain. Tracking down another tip I drove to a different part of the island to an old general store. Yes, even in Kauai! This one was run by a Hawaiian of Japanese descent. As she explained, she was saving the old pieces for her family. However, she laughed recalling the many visiting "mainlanders" who bought the old-store fixtures, from lanterns to storage bins. "They even bought chamber pots," she said, shaking her head in disbelief. I couldn't help but wonder if I had seen any of those things in Indiana, Vermont or Kentucky?

Honolulu, on the island of Oahu, was doing a thriving

antique business. One little section had several shops on one block. There were many art nouveau pieces from jewelry to leaded glass. Bottles, being the big thing in Hawaii, were priced higher than on the mainland— plain, unmarked wine or beer bottles. The dealer explained that the many excavations on the island to build highways and skyscrapers uncovered old bottles. Everybody was collecting. He showed me a book on the subject, *Hawaiian Bottles of Long Ago.* He said most of his stock was brought in regularly from California. Anything that didn't sell after a while was moved away.

I asked another shop owner about finding antique Hawaiian quilts. He shook his head sadly. If he could even find one the price would be five hundred dollars and up.

If you want to know what type of antiques and artifacts are truly Hawaiian, visit the Mission Houses museum and the Iolani Palace. The Mission Houses have items dating back to 1821—American and English china and furnishings. Whatever the missionaries brought or bought at the time. As for the Palace, it's plush, overstuffed Victoriana. So, all of this leaves you to hunt for "Made in Hawaii" bottles or Hawaiian-motif quilts—or the same thing you find at home.

There are garage sales, church rummages, resales, and for the last couple of years, antique shows. Take your time and try your luck while you get a suntan.

Instead of hunting in Europe try antique and collectible searching in less likely countries like Haiti or Jamaica. The advantage is that while antiques have traveled here, and to other out-of-the-way islands, many hunters have not.

Prowling around Port-au-Prince, Haiti, you won't find any shops. That is a good sign. You think, no shops– no dealers. Not quite true.

The dealers climb the mountains to reach Cap Haitien and bring back antiques from decaying plantations. So, there is an antique shop in Cap Haitien at the Mont Jolie Hotel. I have not seen it but other mountain-climbing hunters inform me the things are beautiful and expensive.

Meanwhile down in Port-au-Prince, I made inquiries about church resale shops. Sure enough, at St. Vincent's School for the Handicapped was a resale and antique shop. The nun in charge graciously led me to a large room loaded with French Empire-style furnishings. She explained the dealers brought in many pieces from plantations. Others came from wealthy Haitians cleaning out their garages and servant's quarters. My only purchase was a Capo-di-Monte plate dating early twentieth century, for ten dollars. I bought it more for its souvenir interest than its value. Some magnificent Empire-style beds and buffets were going well under U.S. prices. The problem, of course, would be shipping costs. Sister also showed me some pre-Columbian heads that had been dug up recently on the beach. One was priced at fifty dollars. A magnificent specimen for that kind of money.

So, you see, you can hunt anywhere in the world— and shoot down some bargains in antiques. Just apply the same hunting techniques you would use in your own corner of the world.

Looks almost like an antique shop in Manhattan. It is a stairway to the loft of a resale shop in Jamaica. Chamber pots and other "remnants" of colonialism await antique hunters. The antique shops have many fascinating prints—but not cheap.

Old clocks, church candlesticks, and French porcelain are some of the thrift-shop bargains to be found in Haiti. A magnificent crystal chandelier from a plantation in the hills had just been sold for a fraction of its worth.

A French Empire armoire for a hundred dollars? This one, in excellent condition, is waiting for the traveling antique hunter in Port-au-Prince, Haiti, at a resale shop at St. Vincent School for Handicapped Children. Transportation would up the price however—unless you have a house in Haiti.

Capo-di-Monte from Haiti? This handsome plate or plaque was hanging on a wall in a Port-au-Prince thrift shop for ten dollars. The number on the back and the name "Doccia" showed it wasn't early Capo-di-Monte. Nonetheless, it probably is late nineteenth century and worth more than paid.

Antiques fit for a king fill the bedroom of the late King Kalakala, Hawaiian islands, (1882–86). Many similar period antiques were sold several years ago at an auction of Iolani Palace belongings. They are a conglomerate of European, Oriental, and American Victorian. It is entirely possible your local antique shop may have some of the royal pieces for sale—and not even know about it. Like so many old things, the palace furnishings were not appreciated until they had almost all been sold and scattered. Fortunately, the Iolani Palace Restoration Project is trying to put all of the pieces back together.

—*Courtesy*: Iolani Palace Restoration Project

Many antique shop owners in small towns have pooled their resources and published booklets telling the hunter where they are. Generally, you'll find others unlisted in the same areas. Local Chamber of Commerce offices are the places to find the listings. Also, if you drive, at the state borders.

Small towns, like Friendship, Wisconsin, are fun to go antique and collectible hunting in. Behind every shop counter is an antique price guide. Your best chance is to concentrate, not on bargains, but on finding unusual or "filler" pieces for your collections.

Discoverer and super-collector, Bernie Edwards, with some finds from his "lost stores." All are brand-new antiques—right out of the box. The weird cap on his head was worn by railroaders at the turn of the century. Naturally, he found it in the storeroom for a couple of cents. Unreal, isn't it?

A brand new Charlie McCarthy dummy was unwrapped in the "lost store." The seller didn't think it was worth anything and sold it for a couple of dollars. This may send freaky collectors into convulsions.

A visit to museums like The Barton Museum of Whiskey History are well worth a side trip to Bardstown, Kentucky. Bottle collectors not only get an idea of some rarities to hunt for, but also how the authentic bottles really look.

—*Courtesy*: Barton Museum of Whiskey History

12
Hunting Kitsch Is Chic

THERE IS A thin line between the hunter of nostalgia—
and kitsch. Like the nostalgia seeker, the kitsch hunter
has turned many a former junkman into an antique
gallery owner.

Quantity supersedes quality as the kitsch hunter relentlessly pursues the scent of old railroad nails, metal
shoe-lasts, or Avon bottles. Having the biggest collection of wall-to-wall big-little books and a safe bulging with Orphan Annie decoder pins or first editions of
Superman comics, is the goal.

If one empty beer can is good, two thousand is a
super-staggering collection. Let the world laugh at the

person who spends weekends at the garbage dump or digging into urban renewal sites. That same world will take your collection seriously when you tear out the living-room wall to display a collection. True happiness for this collector is discovering a buried tavern site laden with a mother lode of cans.

As the discoverer, the kitsch hunter automatically becomes an expert. As an expert he can write his own beer-can price guide and appear on national television talk shows. For the truly dedicated kitsch hunter all this personal glory is not enough. The ultimate achievement will be the day he bands together with like-minded kitsch hunters to form a conservation committee. The end is in sight only when the mayor plants a historical marker on the brewery site, declaring it a national monument. Sounds far-fetched? Don't be ridiculous! Keep your eye on the papers and TV. Kitsch marches on!

Consider the hunter of insulators. Track him as he follows the telephone poles to the nearest working telephone repairman. If you're in the desert follow the railroad tracks and you'll spot him. This unlikely path will lead him, and you, too, to old discarded insulators. Presto! a new kitsch collector is launched. That stumpy little glass glob may be worth from fifty dollars and up. What do you do with insulators? Why, you try to see how many you can collect—as cheaply as possible. If anyone doubts your sanity, you just whip out one of the newest kitsch price guides and point to your insulators. See! it's listed and valued at some earthshaking sum!

You can recognize a kitsch hunter any time. He is always in the biggest hurry at garage sales and the most intense. To prove his dedication he has banded together with other kitsch hunters coast to coast, and formed more "clubs" than have antique or nostalgia hunters. Possibly this is because there is more kitsch in various forms than any other collectible. You'll also learn they have newspapers and pen-pal groups. This type of hunter is very sensitive to the slings and arrows cast at his outrageous hunting habits by outsiders. Strangely enough the kitsch hunter is very "straight" and serious. If you don't believe me, test his sense of humor. When he comes charging into the next house-sale, stop him. Tell him you noticed some Beam bottles or fruit jars sticking out of the compost heap in the yard. While he goes plowing up the compost, you will be free to roam, searching for old whisky bottles in the basement. All's fair in antique hunting. Besides, this type of hunter prefers spending as much for ten old fruit jars as one blown-mold flask. The kitsch hunter is so conditioned to looking for kitsch that he wouldn't know an authentic handcrafted antique if he stumbled over one. That is after all not "his thing."

The kitsch hunter will go anywhere in his quest. Follow him out to the old West or the farmlands of Illinois—where men are men. Even the ladies are "into barbed wire" collecting. If you think you might "dig" barbed wire, trek through mud, mire, and scorching deserts. But do it properly armed for the hunt: with heavy boots, gloves, and wire clippers. No danger is too great, from rattlers to quicksand. Let the car rust outdoors while bales of barbed wire are safely stored inside the garage. Comes the next big barbed-wire "swap" and you and it will be out where the action is. Most likely in the middle of the wide-open spaces of Texas.

How do you display a barbed-wire collection? First, you buy a handy-dandy book that lists all varieties. You label and date the bale, and jot down the patent number and place of origin. Then, you snip off an 18-inch strand. This is then mounted on a handsome, polished wood board, or something rustic, along with a sterling silver label. Or, something less fancy, like a gummed paper label. It all depends on the sincerity of the hunter.

The barbed-wire hunter does deserve a hearty slap on the back for being able to find out which is what from the hundreds of types of barbed wire. Give him credit, too, for fighting pollution in his own kinky way. After all, plenty of barbed wire was tossed into rivers and streams. The hunter cleans up whenever he removes old fencing.

The problem is if he doesn't use restraint in his hunting habits. Bales of wire take up a lot of space. However, what are you going to do if you have a couple of thousand feet worth over a hundred dollars per 18-inch strand? And, lots of other hunters anxious to buy or swap! Over two thousand.

Would you believe that there are some opportunists in this world who take full advantage of the kitsch hunter? Somewhere a rumor starts that the W. C. Fields ceramic bourbon bottle is worth two hundred and fifty dollars. Gradually the word reaches a non-collector who owns several liquor stores in a city. Very quietly this dealer buys up as many W. C.'s as he can lay his hands on. Up to this point the bottles have gone up in price ranging from twelve to forty dollars. Not bad for a ceramic bottle widely advertised a couple of years ago when it came out. Now, it is about to be gobbled up by the kitsch hunters. If they are lucky, the housesale conductors and the people who run estate sales will think it is just another quaint, empty bottle— and price it accordingly at around ten dollars.

When W. C. originally came to market, amid great publicity, it was touted only so many would be made. The original mold would then be broken. Now, appropriate time has elapsed for the bottle to be designated a rare "collector's bottle." There are people who do look at their calendars and make such monumental decisions that will influence the lives of kitsch collectors coast to coast.

Kitsch can be very costly. Or, it can be merely over-priced. Take the case of Art Deco. The movement itself began at the Exposition Internationale des Arts Décoratifs et Industriels Modernes in Paris, 1925. The finest designers in every creative field turned out many museum-quality pieces in this highly stylized art form. As you may have gathered, it signaled the unity of the arts with mass production and industry. Names like Le Corbusier, Chanel, Lalique, and Brandt became involved. Clothing, jewelry, architecture, and furniture used this geometric, simple line, combined with stylized flowers, sunrays and lightning bolts. By the time the 1933–34 Chicago World's Fair opened its gates, the entire world was Art Deco or *moderne* mad. Along with the great names in design, everybody got into the act and inexpensive versions of Art Deco could be found in the five-and-ten and Sears Roebuck catalogs. Just for fun, go buy one of the reproduction copies of the 1927 Sears catalog. It's loaded with examples in inexpensive Art Deco. This is the type of Art Deco that appeals to the kitsch hunter.

The antique shops and rummage people are ready and waiting with a wide selection of kitsch Art Deco. A cheap, mass-produced bracelet in Art Deco design or a cigarette box formerly fifty cents are priced from ten dollars up. Regardless of how gross the design, if it is Art Deco, the kitsch collector will pay dearly. Not too long ago boxes of this type and inexpensive costume jewelry were going for nickels and dimes at house and garage sales. Today, they are in boxes labeled "Art

Deco." Gee, you can't even have the fun of sifting through jungles of jewelry anymore!

This is good news for the collectors of well-designed Art Deco. While the kitsch hunter fights another for possession of an Art Deco shoe buckle, the Art Deco fancier will be able to search and possibly find a Baccarat perfume flask or Brandt ash tray of museum quality.

It behooves the hunter of nostalgia and handcrafted antiques to cultivate one or two kitsch hunters. You never know when he will discover an early nineteenth-century sampler or some hand-embroidered pillow-cases. Doubtless you could exchange a Depression-glass plate or some old postcards. Overcome guilt feelings. To the kitsch hunter, he is getting the best of the bargain. You might even throw in a Chicago World's Fair Heinz pickle pin—in mint condition of course.

Are old radios kitsch or nostalgia? It depends probably on what the radios look like. If it is a blue-mirrored circular Sparton, it's Art Deco at its finest. If it is the Philco Baby Grand, it is nostalgia at its finest. But, if it is a collection of super-uglies, with no pretense to design, it's art junko at its finest. Not too long ago every flea market had its share of radios, vintage twenties to forties. Naturally most of them didn't work. However, at the same flea markets there were always sellers with odds and ends of old unused radio tubes. Somehow the kitsch collector put them all together and a new collectible was born. Now, the same hunter will be hard pressed to find tubes or radios at art junko prices.

One enterprising kitsch hunter has used his collection to decorate his restaurant. Everywhere you turn there is an old radio staring you in the face. And, by hunting tubes as well, the radios work for this collector.

Nothing is safe from the kitsch hunter—not even

your old canceled checks. Yes, coins and stamp prices, as well as paper money are not in the kitsch hunter's league. Naturally there is a club called Check Collector's Round Table. And it has over three hundred members. Not just any old canceled check but those with some distinguishing features. Some prefer checks from the 1800s when engraving was finely done. Others search for pictures, inscriptions, and famous names. I don't know about you but I'd be very happy to sell my canceled checks at the first good offer. I have quite a collection of my own. How about trading me one "pay to order of Internal Revenue" for a couple of old valentines? Talk about old checks bouncing back!

Not only is sheer numbers important to kitsch hunter-collectors. Sometimes the weight of their collection arouses envy among their competitors. Consider the fellow who has a really broad card collection that includes bubble-gum and sports cards. It consists of 250,000 cards weighing over a ton.

As any kitsch hunter will tell you, he or she is a historian. Their collections are a catalog of valuable historical items. Who can argue?

Sometimes the kitsch collector becomes so overwhelmed by his collecting habits that he opens a museum. However, to aid fellow hunters he generously offers some of his collection for sale, and charges admission to visitors. Should they buy, the money is applied to their purchase. One such "museum" is operating in Illinois and offers the most marvelous collection of kitsch ever seen. I'm certain this title of "museum" isn't limited to Illinois. In Wisconsin, Tennessee, etc., it generally is known as a curio museum, trading post, or relic museum. They often feature live caged wolves or coyotes.

Sometimes a kitsch collection is practical. One that

falls into this category consists of one hundred and sixty eggbeaters. The collector proudly admits she knows of only one other such collector. Her collection began, appropriately, at a thrift shop with the expenditure of ten cents. However, she is quick to point out that this was no ordinary eggbeater—but one dating circa 1908. From this fabulous find her eggbeater collection was born. Among her prized items is one with an attached glass bowl—of Depression glass. Kudos to her collection. It has nowhere to go but up!

If all of this sounds unbelievable, realize many people are starting to hoard Hula Hoops, Frisbies, and other souvenirs of our plastic age. (Have you tried finding a Hula Hoop lately?) And all because a newspaper story quoted experts in the antique field as saying today's plastic baubles are tomorrow's collectibles. Does it matter they have no aesthetic or functional value? Not to the kitsch collector.

In that great future someday he just knows "it will be worth something." Maybe it will. But, by that time none of us, including him, will be around to cash in on the profits.

Who cares about a Willard or Terry clock when you can own an authentic Colonel Astor, five-cent cigar advertising clock. You'll probably pay just as much or more.

A real find—playing cards from the Chicago World's Fair, 1933–34. Impressive kitsch at the bridge table.

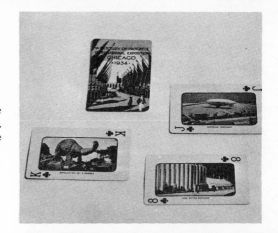

This tin egg from the Columbian Exposition, 1893, can either be kitsch or nostalgia. It depends on your age, I guess. When the egg opens, up pops Columbus on the poop deck of the *Santa Maria.* This could be priced up to fifty dollars— if the collector is desperate.

A W. C. Fields bourbon bottle is a ceramic star in the kitsch world. Value has risen sharply—or shall we say it received a good push. It's priced at two hundred and fifty dollars in some liquor stores. And it's selling! The perfect example of an artificially created "limited edition collector's whatsits."

The kitsch collector even has his own type of silver. These Charlie McCarthy spoons were popular in the 1930s. There were also spoons for the Dionne quintuplets and Mickey Mouse. Since many got thrown away, the remaining pieces are highly collectible—and not cheap.

Ice boxes and coolers of all descriptions are very popular with the kitsch collector. This metal one has an interesting design and could have been purchased at a housesale for twelve dollars. The wooden ones, depending on size, go for from one hundred fifty dollars to three hundred dollars. Let's see—for that three hundred dollars you could also buy a small table or American primitive pieces from the early nineteenth century. To each his own!

What could be more glorious than a genuine Moody Pie advertising sign in your living room? Ultimate happiness—at a price—for the kitsch collector.

A toy car to gladden the heart of the freaky collector. This one was found in the "lost store" by hunter Bernie Edwards.

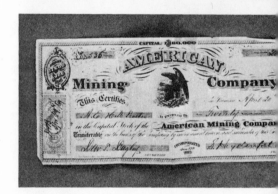

Old mining stock certificates are still not too expensive. They turn up in attics with old love letters, etc. The kitsch collector's chance to own his own silver and gold mines.

A chicken hatchery (incubator) in the dining room? Just the thing to hold the Charlie McCarthy silver, etc. This genuine redwood incubator has its original copper heating unit—just in case. I found this one for five dollars at a garage sale. Similar pieces go for up to fifty dollars. The glass door lifts up and there is storage space behind it for magazines—or silver.

13

What Happens When the Hunt Is at Your Place?

Is THERE ANYONE in the United States who hasn't had a sale in their own garage, basement, or yard? By now many of these amateurs have turned pro. They have professionally printed garage-sale signs furnished by local real-estate firms, and keep mailing lists like regular housesale conductors.

For the novice, having your own house or garage sale isn't just a matter of fun and profit. None of the experts who write about how to have house and garage sales tell it like it is. Actually there is something positively frightening about a line of strangers waiting outside your home, armed with shopping bags.

Rule 1: Don't do it by yourself. "Misery loves company" is no idle quote. Plus, there are certain side benefits to sharing a garage or basement—when it's someone else's.

You'll find it much easier to carry a few hundred items than to make continuous pots of coffee and sandwiches, and later, drinks and buffet, for your fellow sellers. Also, sharing space means sharing the cost of running an ad and having the best money changers of the group in charge.

Consider what can possibly happen when you do it yourself.

Those people snorting and pawing the ground with their sneakers and boots aren't just ordinary human beings. They have followed the scent of antiques and collectibles to *your* doorstep. You are alone on the other side of the door. If your door doesn't open promptly at the advertised second they tend to become unruly, even menacing. Possibly the day before you have been deluged by phone calls and people knocking on your front door, cajoling or threatening you to let them in before the sale. Do you have the bravery and courage to let them in before the sale? Do you have the bravery and courage to roar back? Don't be intimidated or all may be lost. A favorite trick of the battle-hardened dealers is to arrive the day before the sale and claim the ad said the sale was that day. Abuse follows if you refuse entry. Be wary of the charming man or woman who is overly polite and arrives the day before. "Oh, we were just passing through town and won't be back this way tomorrow," is a favorite ploy. Fortunately you recognize them; they have an antique booth at the local flea market year round. Another excuse for early hunting runs, "Oh, can't I just take a tiny peek at what you are

selling? Then I'll know if I want to come back."
Once they get their foot in the door the game is over
for you. If they are dealers (and undoubtedly they
are) they'll begin making derisive remarks about what
you're selling and that it is overpriced. If you are foolish
enough to let them in, in the first place, don't let them
intimidate you. It helps if you have a large dog chained
in the next room.

In the dim past of fifteen years ago my husband
decided we should sell just a few things to raise money
for a pet project. We ran the ad in the newspaper and
had exactly two replies. Visitor one wasn't the least bit
interested in what we were selling. Instead, he looked
over every inch of our apartment, without moving. It
occurred to us he was casing the place for a future visit.
Our second callers introduced us to the fabled Hotfinger family. While one professed interest in the china
we were selling, the second one asked to use our bathroom. Since there wasn't anything in there, I pointed
out the direction. Mrs. Hotfinger meantime was arguing
over prices. Then she diverted my husband's attention
to an object on the other side of the room. In that split
second his expensive lighter disappeared. During the
exchange we *lost* some change. The Hotfingers had
struck again. Not for several years did I see them. But
I learned they were well known. Legally I found you
can't prevent Hotfingers from coming to a general
housesale when other strangers are also coming. Nor
can you accuse them unless you catch them in the act.
Imagine my horror when they showed up five years
later at my first honest-to-goodness basement sale.

In my advertisement I had mentioned antiques, as
well as miscellaneous. At five in the morning of the sale
day my phone rang. It was Max the Picker. By then I
had become somewhat acquainted with the various
characters in the antique business. Max had a distinc-

tive voice—rude and unpleasant. Who can be friendly at that hour, you may ask. Who would even call at that hour—but Max? He wanted to know if he could come over at seven that morning. Naturally he was indignant when I slammed the phone down. At least I had learned something from my early Hotfinger days.

Meanwhile, the cars began lining up outside my house, and around the block. Faces peered at me through my dining-room window. Two people climbed the fence. Among the crowd I spotted my old friends, the Hotfingers. Nervously, I did the only thing that came to mind. I phoned one of my neighbors who has a deputy sheriff's badge and told him to hurry over.

He came, and dramatically wore his badge and also carried a revolver in a holster under his coat. It was all very exciting. I pointed out the Hotfingers and he decided he would follow them around and make them too nervous to lift anything. You may not have to go to such drastic lengths.

The moment arrived, and in the buyers charged, pushing and yelling at each other. Two people grabbed an old patchwork quilt and tugged at opposite ends. My friend the sheriff interceded. The crowd descended upon a table covered with small glass and china pieces. When they turned away the table had been picked nearly bare. Swell, from my point of view! I guess the prices were super-low. Also, I used this as a big opportunity to get rid of Nippon and late pieces of pressed glass (1900s) that I wasn't interested in.

The first group dashed away clutching copies of sale pages of the local paper and mumbling about "there's a good one over on Fourth Street." Aside from a few little items like a single drawer knob, bottle stopper, and souvenir spoon, nothing had been lifted. The take was over a hundred dollars in about one hour.

This gave me false encouragement. Obviously, I thought, my fortune was about to be made. This was a mistaken idea. The biggest crush came in the morning and then just before closing time.

Rule 2: Remember that dealers hunt in packs. They "do" the most promising sales first and at the end of the day scan the papers for last-minute possibilities.

The rest of the day moved very slowly. Mothers with baby buggies; mothers with small children. They came looking mostly for practical items—clothing, basinettes and toys. About three o'clock the over-forty crowd dribbled in. They were mostly lookers. "Oh, remember when I had one of those castor sets?" one would say. Or, "Look how much this cane-bottom chair is. I have one just like it."

Just before closing time quite a few men came looking for machinery and old tools—or new tools.

Chalk up another fifty dollars for six hours of work. This made the grand total one hundred and fifty or so dollars. It was one hundred and fifty dollars I didn't have before, right?

Rule 3: Keep in mind that the dealers arrive first. They don't want to pay retail prices. So, don't put out all of the most desirable antiques first. Save at least a few items for mid-morning and late afternoon. The dealers will always come back to talk a price down if they see something they want. Another benefit from having a joint sale with friends is that they may have something you want.

Rule 4: Many times fellow sellers aren't necessarily astute hunters. You may find a "sleeper."

At my first joint venture with four other sellers we all averaged about a hundred dollars apiece. Not much was left and we were bone weary when closing time came. In fact, one friend decided to leave an old rocking chair priced at four dollars in my garage. As time passed I forgot about the rocker. After all, it was covered with peeling blue paint and some of the seat had disintegrated. My friend called and asked if I would want to buy it for four dollars. It was just too much trouble to lug it back to her basement. Big-hearted me accepted her offer. Only then did I take a closer look at the rocker. Even with the cruddy paint the acorn finials and splint seat shouted "Shaker" at me. Grabbing a piece of sandpaper I worked anxiously on the leg. A score line appeared. Stripped of the old paint finish and redone with an oil-wax finish it was indeed an early Shaker rocker. Later, my friend told me she had bought it in the East twenty years ago for a dollar fifty at auction. Meanwhile, in a recent Vermont auction a similar chair went for two hundred dollars.

Rule 5: If you spot something great at your sale that a friend is selling, don't show any enthusiasm. Let's say an old chest of drawers has been gathering mold in Sally L's basement for years. She has finally decided to part with it for fifteen dollars. None of the others seem interested in it. But, you take a closer look. It appears to be Victorian with inlay work on the drawers. The yellow paint and daisy decals obscure the natural finish. Don't squeal "Sally, do you know what this is?" and then try to buy it. Her reaction will automatically be to call across the street and have her husband take it back home. You have just helped her rediscover a family heirloom. This also automatically puts the others on standby alert as far as the other goodies are concerned. There is usually a flurry of marking up the prices or trucking things back home. Silence can be golden if you would be lucky at your own housesale.

The Pitfall Pricing Syndrome traps many unwitting sellers. However, if you are lucky, you can also catch a few hunters. Well-meaning friends who consider themselves experts on every subject will offer you pricing advice. They will base their price tags on the following reasoning:

1. Anything that is an antique is valuable and therefore should have a high price tag.

2. Anything that is currently a popular collectible will garner cash.

Currently anything that is oak furniture, regardless of how ugly, is super-expensive. Generally because it has an "old" appearance and hints of art nouveau or Victorian, the would-be seller will snatch at the bait without a thorough examination of the object.

An oak combination cabinet-desk-bookcase that originally was a prize-winning design at the 1893 Columbian Exposition is making multiple appearances in shops, garage sales, etc. The top price I have seen is three hundred and eighty-five dollars. This one has a convex glass door and is rather attractive. Possibly it was made shortly after its twin won a prize. The second group of oak desk combos is of 1927 vintage. You'll find it pictured on page 905 of the 1927 Sears Roebuck catalog. An ugly beastie it is.

Hunter's Tip: Buy a copy of the newly reproduced 1927 Sears catalog. It is a reference guide no dedicated hunter should be without. Not only will you find 1927 golden-oak furniture, but hundreds of Empire, Victorian, and cane-seat chairs. To a new hunter they might look a hundred years older than they are. Especially under a dim garage lightbulb. Now, if that oak bookcase circa 1927 is priced for twenty-five dollars, it's a buy. At a hundred and fifty dollars it isn't.

Before you go price-tagging your objects, at least figure out if they are authentic. If reproduced, when— 1890s or yesterday?

A friend who knows everything about everything advised another seller to put a high price on what appeared to be Empire pieces in very bad condition. A collection of fruit jars of the common aqua variety were also priced high—"because they are popular." At the end of the day the jars and furniture were still there. The seller did a hot business on odds and ends—a saucer here, a bowl there. Of course, on another day she might have sold the Empire and fruit jars. It's very "iffy."

Sometimes you have to use a little salesmanship to get the sale moving. Encourage several friends who are not involved to come over and show great enthusiasm for those old decks of playing cards, monogrammed cocktail napkins, and the ice buckets. If you are lucky you'll have buyers fighting over them; sometimes even upping the price. Nothing dishonest—just enthusiastic. Little comments—"Well, if you don't want it, I'll buy it"— often work wonders with the buyer considering a purchase. Or, they may say, "It's yours."

I generally find it isn't a good idea to label anything. Don't identify the hat-pin holder as "Victorian hat-pin holder," or the pressed-glass bowl as "early pressed glass." Not only could you be wrong, but people prefer to think they are making their own discovery. Let them find the Imari dish or the school desk circa 1890 and put their own labels on it. You can depend on it—they'll ask you if something is old. It is better to say that you don't know the vintage. No long dissertations, please. If you tell them something is crudola circa 1890 and it isn't, chances are they'll either bring it back or think you are dishonest.

Rule 6: To mark down or not to mark down prices is a weighty question.

Often you'll find the second-time-arounders stopping by one minute before you begin dividing up the profits. They'll offer to take many things off your hands—for half price or more. Sometimes they'll even come back the following day in the hopes something they wanted to buy is still unsold. Generally, it seems like a great opportunity to get rid of the kitsch—the old clothes, bowling balls, and wooden golf clubs—once and for all. Unfortunately if they are dealers, that isn't always what they have in mind. They are thinking more in terms of the Rookwood planter or silver napkin rings. There is no point in letting honest antiques and collectibles go at give-away prices. Save them for another day. Or, you may decide to collect them in quantity yourself. The ideal situation is the "junker" who comes back and offers to take everything left (except the antiques and collectibles) for a few dollars. You have three choices:

1. Save the remains for church rummage and a tax deduction.
2. Swap junk for junk with your friends.
3. Let the junker carry it away.

Whatever you do—don't put it back in the basement.

How many garage or housesales can you have a year? Apparently, there can be too much of a good thing in certain suburban communities. Many have passed ordinances stating no more than two sales a year for any person in single-family dwellings. This came about because many people living in two-hundred-thousand-dollar homes take a dim view of having hoards of strangers trampling their shrubbery and using their driveways to reach a neighbor's garage sale.

Rule 7: Check village or community ordinances to find out about parking and selling on your block. If you have too many sales you might also note the IRS among the browsers, taking notes. Income is taxable, you know. One couple does a thriving business selling sales samples and surplus along with the wife's last year's wardrobe. This pads their income nicely, and who would ever miss those boxes of dinnerware or light fixtures?

Another approach is to make the rounds of garage sales for several months, going at the final closing moments. Then you can put it all together for double the purchase price at you own gala. This, my dears, accounts for the strangely familiar look of so many antiques and collectibles at garage sales. They move from place to place. Who knows, *you* may even end up buying back something you sold last year!

Did you ever go hunting in your own house? A couple I know who are inveterate do-it-yourselfers made some fascinating discoveries remodeling their old farmhouse. While knocking out walls they discovered a hidden room. Apparently the house had been added onto three times, dating back to the Civil War. Whoever had done the first remodeling job had found it easier to simply "wall up" one room and a staircase. The worker or workers didn't bother to do much of a clean-up job. When the couple uncovered the room, they also came across an old whisky bottle, wooden ice skates and a Civil War belt buckle. Further along they pulled out a child's shoes, newspapers, and an old parasol. I shouldn't be at all surprised if they gradually tear the whole house apart, hunting for other antiques. No sacrifice is too great for the hunter.

Every garage sale seems to have an old sewing machine base, piano bench, and crocks. These aren't the hot sellers they were several years ago. The patient hunter can find them at bargain prices. Also popular are picture frames and empty wine jugs, circa 1970. The jugs are popular with horticulturists for making miniature gardens under glass. So drink up and sell your empties for a quarter apiece. Artists have discovered that garage sale picture frames are more interesting— and cheaper—than the new ones.

Customers at garage sales come in all ages. You never know, after the first surge of hunters, whether the rest of the day will go as well. Strangely enough, most hunters don't realize they can do better at a privately held sale than a conducted one. Things at this sale were really priced "to sell." The problem with most sellers is that they expect retail prices for their junk. When it doesn't sell, they wonder why.

These pressed-gass bowls, circa 1930–40, were staples at most garage sales till recently. In the good old days they went for nickels and dimes. Suddenly you can get up to a dollar or more.

Surprising things can turn up at your own garage sale—when you hold it with several others. Play it cool when you spot a yellowware bowl like this one, priced at fifty cents.

Where can you find a silver-plated hand mirror in an art nouveau design these days for a few dollars? This turn-of-the-century piece was doubtless part of a three-piece set. As a single, it will do nicely in a powder room for guests.

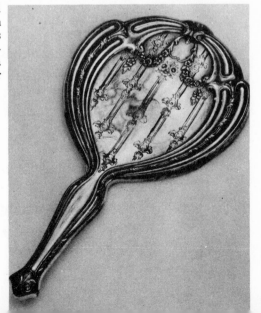

14
Hunting for an Antiques Guru

It is only natural that the antique hunter seek words of wisdom and encouragement from a wise, experienced antiques' sage. Springing up to meet the need are gurus who teach classes in antiques and art. From coast to coast, collectors can be found worshipping at the feet of these self-proclaimed teachers. I say "self-proclaimed" because you and I could become antique gurus by merely running an advertisement inviting people to our classes.

Many gurus are indeed knowledgeable in the field. But they are hard to find. It's no use asking students about their gurus. Their judgment is clouded by reverence. What then is a hunter to do? Why is one guru proper and another not? Who is a guru?

Try to find a teacher who does not sell art or antiques himself. Now I realize that dealers must live like everybody else. And, many are qualified to teach. But, there is something a bit underhanded about snaring a roomful of bright-eyed novice collectors and selling them your antiques. This comes about several ways.

Some classes offer "home study groups" in the dealer's home. Sound logical? Why not learn surrounded by the teacher's private collection? Naturally the students find it hard to resist the opportunity to buy when all these wonders are dangled under their noses. Let's say the subject for the evening is pressed glass. And the examples used for the show-and-tell session are owned by the teacher. How generous and good-hearted of the great guru to allow the student to buy pieces of his choice. So convenient.

One guru is heavy into art prints, etchings, and engravings. Not only does he have a shop "by appointment only," but once a month he auctions off his collections. His classes are held in a very fancy suburb. His students pick up "status" art for fancy auction prices. No matter the Rembrandt etching is phony. The guru says he "thinks it's a Rembrandt" and therefore it is fact. It's better than playing backgammon all the time and more exciting than needlework. Besides, his students don't really care if they are buying reproductions or fakes. What counts is they are buying from their guru.

Many gurus get their foot in the door by teaching first at the local adult evening classes in high schools. Unfortunately, you can't sit in before you pay your money. However, you can ask one of the students a simple question: *Does the guru sell antiques?*

Several reputable and qualified teachers come to my mind. They are from different parts of the country. But they have several important points in common.

1. They began as collectors and spent much time researching.
2. They don't sell antiques.
3. They may appraise for local historical societies and museums.
4. They may appraise as a service.

Perhaps it seems a thin line of differentiation between selling and appraising. Both have a service to sell. Yet, that thin line makes the difference between an objective point of view and one with self-interest behind it.

It is possible for the teacher to be a dealer and be a good teacher. Better if he isn't.

Many collectors band together, then seek out a guest "lecturer" once a month for their teach-ins. This may be another collector, a recognized authority, or a museum affiliate.

Sometimes within a group of collectors one will do a great deal of research on, say, Canton china, and report his findings to the others. This seems to work quite well for bottle collectors and the Oriental Art Society. The show-and-tell portion of the class or meeting is one of the best ways to learn about antiques and art.

Guru Hunter's Tip: Ask various teachers if they use the show-and-tell method. It takes a really good guru to be able to point out what's what with a wide range of objects.

The guru should supplement the classes with special trips to museums and restorations. A trip to Williamsburg or Greenfield Village, or the decorative arts department of the Metropolitan—or your local equivalents

—is an invaluable tool for any hunter. The guru himself should be knowledgeable enough to point out details that help the hunter recognize an authentic antique or art print when he comes face to face with one in somebody's basement or attic. This also puts individual antiques in their proper period and setting. And you can say, "Oh, is that what that was used for?" These guided tours should inspire any hunter to spend his time searching for handcrafted pieces. Not because they are so valuable, but for the sheer appreciation of a handcrafted object.

Classes are a great mind opener. The good guru asks his students questions. And, they are forced to reason why a silver spoon isn't the antique it is supposed to be. One class I took began with every student being an expert. It ended with them all being aware, but not certain, until the proper proof was presented.

Guru Hunter's Tip: The good guru will teach the hunter not to accept things on face value—or anybody's word. The student learns that it is important for him to rely on his own judgment.

The cost of classes can vary from a school quarter of lectures for twenty-five dollars, plus extra for tours, to a series for fifty dollars. Perhaps it's less where you live.

Beware the guru who makes snap financial judgments on objects during the show-and-tell time. Remember, face-value judgments don't always hold up. For instance, you bring a bowl to class with a crossed-sword mark on the bottom. The guru who makes a snap judgment and says, "It's Meissen, very old, very valuable," may be leading you astray. The fact is there have been subtle changes in the Meissen markings over the years, especially with the popular blue-onion porcelain. Is it old or new? Authentic or fake? From 1724 to 1934 the crossed swords were longer or shorter or added tiny brush strokes. It requires a bit of expertise and not an instant glance to pinpoint Meissen—and most other pieces. Is your Martha Washington worktable the original or one of the reproductions made over the years? Hopefully your guru will know for sure, and explain how you, too, will know.

One of the important lessons the hunter can learn is how to research in the library or build up his own antique reference library. On the night you study porcelain or silver, the good guru will have several of the books on marks and history of patterns. The books are passed among the class. The guru selects a piece of porcelain or silver and after the class examines it, the class must look up the date marks or identifying marks in the books. Yet, you too can learn how to read a date mark.

Another helpful teaching technique is to use color slides of historical rooms and the antiques in them. Here again antiques are visually placed in their natural settings.

A subject I have yet to see discussed in the classroom would identify the different woods and then relate them to the country and date when they were used. Maybe somebody will research a reference book on woods used at different times in history.

Every hunter needs all the help he can get. And while help abounds in libraries and museums, most hunters have a hard time going by themselves to the library or museum. It's much easier—and more fun—to do it with your antiques class. The spirit of friendly competition between students encourages more rapping about the hows and whys of antiques. You also realize you aren't so unusual collecting inkwells after all. So do two other classmates. It's even more fun to discover several dealers "incognito" taking notes like crazy.

As students progress they become eligible for the advanced classes. These usually cover one category—furniture, glass, or whatever is currently a trend. Probably Art Deco classes are being included in some courses. There should be side trips to observe the restoration of antiques. What a Chippendale chair looks like stripped down, with maybe a leg in traction. This is an opportunity to take a close look at all of the parts—mortises, nails, etc.

The joyous part comes when you leave your guru to go out into the world. And you realize you don't know as much as you thought you did. In fact, it is a bit of comfort knowing that neither you nor anyone is really a total expert. It is a constant learning process.

If there isn't a study group in your area, start your own. You'd be amazed how much you can learn from other people's mistakes—and opinions as well as your own.

Old catalogs are a fantastic source of reference for Victorian objects as well as Art Deco. Many of the old trade catalogs have been discovered and reissued. This goes for toy catalogs as well as Montgomery Ward and Sears Roebuck.

Be your own guru. The catalogs may give you proper definitions for such oddities as a collar-button box, roll-plate vest chains, and emery bags. You'll find some things aren't as old as you imagined (mail-order spinning wheels), and some things aren't as new (celluloid objects).

Hairpieces and wigs for women are to be found in an 1895 catalog—along with beards, mustaches, and wigs for men. You never know when you might run across an antique beard at a housesale. Thanks to your catalog studies you may recognize it before the other hunters. Presto! a new collectible craze begins.

Not too long ago a question came up in the local antiques class about a pressed-glass compote. Even the guru thought the compote dated circa 1920. Because of the particular pattern another student proved it was an 1895 piece. She found it in her Ward's catalog—dating it without a doubt.

Would you know aquatint from a mezzotint? A good guru will explain the difference. This aquatint by French artist Vernet was done in 1850 and found in a resale shop for twelve dollars. The guru will tell you whether it is a reprint or the real thing. There is no trick to making reprints if the skilled printer has an old plate. An engraver can rework the old plate, re-engraving the old lines. Obviously this takes time—and accounts for the cost of good reprints. Many can be reworked this way on old paper. An experienced hunter can tell the difference. The novice needs a guru.

Is your jug really a Toby jug? If so, how did it get its name? What is it worth today? The factual side of antiques is what you should expect to learn in a well-taught antiques class. The teacher should preferably not be a dealer—with wares to sell. Guru Leonard Weinzimmer (right) is the ideal teacher. He appraises for museums and galleries and teaches evening classes in between. The high point of his classes is the show-and-tell technique. Students bring their treasures to be discussed and identified.

You've just bought a genuine Rookwood sculptured bud vase for a dollar at a basement sale. Is it a vellum finish worth over a hundred dollars? Excitedly you decide to show it to your guru. It is signed on the bottom with the Rookwood flames and roman numerals adding up to twenty-two. There is also an "X" imprinted. Your guru tells you it isn't a vellum but a matte finish. It was made in 1922 and the "X" means it's imperfect. Nevertheless, to a Rookwood collector it will have a value of more than the dollar you paid.

Was this majolica dish made in England, America, or Italy? Or is it a reproduction? A good guru will tell you all about the history of majolica and why this is an American piece. Majolica was first exhibited in England in 1851 by Minton at the London Exhibition. Shortly thereafter, American potters copied this rather crude earthenware with its molded designs. It wasn't really respectable with collectors until the last few years. Some of it is pretty ugly but it is just as expensive now as an attractive piece. This green-and-white dish cost fifty cents at a garage sale.

Nineteenth-century match safes often turn up behind old basement doors, where they were hung to have matches handy to light furnace fires. This one had peeling yellow paint and sold for twenty-five cents at a basement sale. Underneath the paint was a metal match holder valued at twenty-five dollars. They were handsome, ornate pieces of cast iron.

Your guru will probably tell you not to sneer at twentieth-century American pewter. The restoration of colonial Williamsburg in Virginia in the 1920s brought back the popularity of pewter. Many of the new copies of early American pieces are turning up at garage and housesales. Some of the hallmarks of twentieth-century pieces read "pewter." The antiques didn't say anything about materials. Some names of pewter companies are Insico, Puritan, Wilcox, American S. P. Co., and Rice. These pieces are quite attractive—and cheap. Just let your guru tell you how to distinguish the old from the new.

15

Hunting for Your House

LEARN TO RESIST the lure of buying at every sale; even a conducted sale that offers "four floors of Victorian mansion bulging with goodies." Greed is one of the worst enemies of the hunter. Before you go charging off, your nose pointed toward the scent, stop and ask yourself, "What am I hunting for? Do I really need another demitasse cup or rocking chair?"

Hunt with a purpose. Analyze what you are hunting and collecting all that stuff for. Will your trophies be willed to a museum? Are you going to start your own museum? Are the heirlooms for your family something that they will want? Are your collecting habits strictly for status? Do you hope to sell all for hard cash and head for Tahiti? Or, do you simply hunt for your home and lifestyle, and hang the historical significance! Maybe when you go out on a hunting expedition you are looking for a chair to suit your son's room, a lamp for the den, old pipes for your husband's collection, or cookware for the kitchen. The haphazard or greedy hunter will only end up with the makings of a junk shop.

Hunter's Tip: Don't be sidetracked by fad collecting. What is currently popular and overpriced should be avoided. Reroute your thinking and ask, "Do I need it? Do I really like it?" Or, "If I think it is ghastly, can I sell it to someone else for a profit?"

Even though you really can survive without buying one more thing for your house, you head for that Victorian housesale. Cars, campers, and U-hauls line the streets. You have to park five blocks away. Obviously it's too late to find anything worthwhile. Nevertheless you trudge onward. It will be fun to see what was for sale and how much it was priced at. Probably you couldn't afford it anyhow. As you enter, all the old familiar faces are there, including Fat Flora and her hunting companion, Greasy Oscar. They are putting a closed bid on a monstrous three-piece bedroom set with a six-foot-high headboard. At present, the price tag reads three thousand dollars. And to think a few years ago you could hardly give this type of Victoriana away! You eavesdrop and learn that Fat Flora is making a bid on it for fifteen hundred dollars. She tell Greasy Oscar she has a customer waiting in the wings who will pay three thousand.

Hunter's Tip: Closed bids are a good idea if you can afford to take the chance of maybe winning, or maybe losing. Just for fun try an absurdly low bid. Sometimes it works—if the seller is anxious enough to get rid of the object.

Meanwhile, you see several pieces of late Empire furniture priced from three hundred dollars for a super-ugly chest of drawers to five hundred dollars for a table with animal feet. All are tagged sold. Apparently anything goes if it is classified antique. Or, housesale fever is running rampant and anything goes. There are wall-to-wall people pushing their way to the cashier buying everything in sight. As the dust settles you see nothing is left except some 1930s heavy modern furniture. You are almost the only person without a purchase. Then you see it—alone and unenticing, near the cashier's table. Strangely it has no sale tag on it. Small, almost black, stands a spinet desk in darkly stained walnut. Pushing through the crowd you take a closer look. The price is an unbelievable fifteen dollars. Why is it still for sale? Anyone can see its graceful Federal legs and pigeonhole compartments. The fact that it is a small piece should make it more desirable. Apparently this is not the day for anything but monster antiques. A nineteenth-century antique that would sell for up to fifty dollars was in fair condition for fifteen—and no takers. Possibly, the dealers thought it was one of the spinet desks reproduced in 1927. Close examination would have revealed the joining wood at the inner corners as typical of the early nineteenth century. Noticing your interest one of the dealers laughingly nudges you, saying, "Too bad you didn't get here early when the old stuff was still here." You pay the fifteen dollars and lug the desk outside. In the daylight you note the piece had been sitting in a basement or attic for a long time. The bottoms of the legs and the back have thick dust and water or dampness stains. Once home it responds to a clean-up with flax soap and lemon oil. And, it fills the need for a small worktable-desk in your son's bedroom. Perfect size for a typewriter.

When you hunt for your house consider your life-style. If you are an innovator with an eclectic eye, Victorian silver pieces, mixed and matched, have new uses. For many years it was cheap and plentiful. It wasn't appreciated or in the same class with Georgian silver—still isn't with purists. But Victorian silver plate made toward the end of the nineteenth century has a charm all its own. I thought it would be fun to mix a bowl or plate with the stark lines of my contemporary silver. My requirements included serving pieces, flat-ware or whatever struck my fancy—and was inexpen-sive. (Have you priced new silver lately?) It is well to remember that at most housesales the silver is polished up and priced up. Often it is put in a special room. Usually it disappears very fast. However, there is al-ways another sale and another chance. My opportunity came at a garage sale. The grandchildren of an elderly Swedish woman were disposing of pieces of furniture, china, silver, and textiles they had no interest in. The fine sterling silver had been sold to dealers before the garage sale, they said. The remaining pieces were dis-played on card tables in the backyard. Two blackened serving pieces caught my attention. One, a shell-shaped dish about eight inches in length, was priced at four dollars. The other, a very heavy tray, was marked twelve dollars. I wasn't really quite sure what I would find under the tarnish. Luckily both pieces polished up to a beautiful gleam and proved to be Victorian electro-plated silver.

If you like to entertain large groups of people buffet style and are loath to use plastic eating utensils, get acquainted with the dozens of pieces of Victorian flat-ware designed specially for everything from soup to fish. Why fuss if you can't afford a 24-piece setting in your silver pattern? Instead, shop the sales for a fish or fruit set; a meat fork and a butter knife for fifty cents or less each. The ornate patterns are great fillers and add interest to a buffet table. It doesn't even matter if they match. Or, if you have one fruit knife with one fish fork—they are similar enough to get along well. They also make a summer picnic more elegant. If you accidently lose one, chances are you can always find another at the next garage sale. The tiny fruit knives, some with pearl handles, can be perfect for hors d'oeuvres. Other long-forgotten pieces are ice-cream forks, oyster servers, food pushers, and olive forks. If they are cheap enough, you can always find a use for them.

Silver baby cups, rattles, and napkin rings are harder to come by. Keep your eyes open and discover an unusual gift for that new baby. Or, save it for your own family.

Even a silver pitcher or bowl with a hole in the bottom can be a find—if cheap enough. And, if you like the looks of it, stuff yours with a plant or two and a fake bottom.

Silver-plated vanity sets (mirror, comb, and brush) turn up as singles at many an attic sale. Especially interesting for your powder room are those with the art nouveau designs. Don't pass one by just because it has a monogram on it. Who will ever know it wasn't a past family member's initial!

The late Victorian period popularized gold and silver plated pieces, often combined with cut glass. The small, footed jewelry boxes in metal are handsome accessories for powder rooms—as minisoap containers. Or, for your luggage keys or hairpins. I found a cut-glass humidor with gold plated top at an antique show. It was priced low because the seller didn't know exactly what it was. Now it holds cotton balls as a decorative bathroom accent. You might use yours for its original intention—cigars.

Some of the best housesale buys that go unnoticed are textiles, with the exception of crazy quilts and patchwork quilts. Embroidered pillow cases as well as collars, cuffs, and doilies edged in lace can be converted to company, guestroom, or party use. Even dresser scarves, long out of fashion, can be shorn of their handmade laces. The lace can then be added to plain pillow cases. While a large damask table cloth still commands a goodly price, small round and square cloths may be yours for a dollar. Use them to dress up the humble card table—for a large, seated dinner party. Consider buying damaged napkins and clothes edged with lace and embroidery. Chop them up and rework them into fancy napkins; or framed under glass they can be treated as an art form.

One antique dealer has been doing a thriving business with damaged Oriental robes. While I don't recommend it, she has chopped them up and framed them under glass in oblongs of four-by-eight inches. A section of a sleeve, with embroidered designs, becomes a wall decoration. In a sense these new ways with old objects are acceptable—the preservation of handwork. Old watch parts have long been turned into collages.

Rag-tag books with missing and loose pages may seem a total waste of money at first glance. Not so. The old steel engravings, especially in children's books, can be used for decoupage. When you can purchase an entire book for fifty cents, how can you go wrong? A plain toy box becomes a charming piece of furniture, treated to the discarded pages of a Charles Dickens' book or Victorian children's book. If you aren't interested, consider gifting a friend with some choice selections for her decoupaging.

While you're looking through those old books, you may come across some advertising trade cards stuck between the pages. Some cards feature Mother Goose characters and quaintly dressed children. Several, framed, could be a gift to a friend who collects them.

Wallpaper is expensive. Use old book pages, theater bills, and newspapers for wall coverings. The same use applies to old sheet music. So you see, hunting for the house can sometimes be the nickels-and-dimes project.

A friend found an old folding screen lying in an alley. All it needed to bring it back to life were a couple of hinges and the application of some of those book pages she had lying around.

Budget Hunter's Tip: There's scarcely an antique item that can't be converted from trash to "decor." See what you can find for a few cents. It may not be a valuable antique, but it does have a use.

Baskets of all shapes and sizes show up at give-away prices in basements and garages. The prettiest can be interesting plant containers. Sometimes small Oriental baskets with covers can become kitchen helpers. I have two, about three inches in diameter, with well-ventilated weave. They cost ten cents each in bright blue and red. Because of their wide weave they hold shallots, ginger, garlic, or chili pods on my kitchen shelves. Larger versions, often with a ring of Peking glass as handle, appear at flea markets. There they are priced from eight to twenty dollars. Keep looking. You'll eventually spot one much cheaper in someone's attic. This larger size holds paper napkins or small kitchen tools.

Old lighting devices, even without wicks and glass shades, are a must for any home. When the power fails, you can quickly light up. They come in so many shapes, sizes, and materials you can just about choose your favorite. They are expensive in shops—from thirty dollars up.

There are times when it is wise to hunt in an antique shop—from the most reputable dealer you know of. This is especially true when hunting for your own house. This is different than general hunting or hunting for a collection. It is more personal—and something that will be handed down in your family.

Small antiques that are slightly different in purpose or appearance fall into the "good buy" category. One of my favorite house finds was discovered in a very expensive antique gallery. It was an early nineteenth-century inlaid-wood jewelry box. It has a practical use and represented an antique that doesn't show up very often—anywhere. With the exception of a missing escutcheon and key, it was in beautiful condition. The price seemed staggering to me at the time. After all, I could have purchased a handsome, brand-new jewelry box, complete with music box, for less. However, the box goes with my antique furnishings as well as serving a practical purpose. Even more to the point—it has doubled in value since I bought it. There simply aren't enough Georgian jewelry boxes around.

I've even learned to love a *poudreuse*—for a couple hundred dollars. It is the only piece of antique furniture I have ever purchased from a dealer. When I saw it I didn't even know its proper name was *poudreuse*. It looked like a dressing table or vanity, with a hinged mirror inside its lid. With the top down it was a small bedside table with a drawer and shelf for holding a phone or storing cosmetics. This was no ordinary dressing table. While it wasn't a Louis XV, it was completely inlaid with tiny marquetry squares on the outside— from case to legs. Birdseye maple on the inside. The outwardly curving legs combined the marquetry work with an ebony stain. Still, it represented a substantial investment. Why not add a couple hundred more dollars (on handy time payments) and buy an American primitive cherry table, or less for a pine dry sink? It seemed then, and now, that the purchase of an uncommon piece would lend more interest to my bedroom. When, if ever, would I come across this early Victorian powder table, and this beautiful marquetry design? I'm happy to say in the five years since I found it, I haven't seen another. There are many Queen Anne types and Colonial copies. The number of man hours required to do this marquetry work by hand in order to reproduce it wouldn't be worth the asking price. So, thanks to a dealer, I have a unique antique for my home. The dry sink and cherry table have of course gone up in price. But there is always the chance of finding them in a basement or attic for a few dollars.

Hunter's Tip: Look for the uncommon piece when hunting in antique shops. Even at shop prices they are a wise investment.

One of the most expensive outlays for the house can be the floor coverings. This is when the housesale is the answer to a hunter's prayer. Rarities of museum-quality Oriental rugs and even prayer rugs turn up at a fraction of the current cost. Check first to see what good Orientals are going for in stores and at dealers'. Many hundreds to thousands of dollars. If you take the time to study an Oriental rug book and visit the finer stores, you will prepare for the great rug hunt. Just be sure the rug is in good condition. Often the small rugs turn up for from twenty-five to forty dollars. A large 9 x 14 footer will probably cost you three hundred or more at a housesale. That same rug would possibly be priced for several thousand at a dealer's. For a while everybody was "hot" on Orientals and dealers would stand in line in subzero weather at a housesale advertising Orientals. Now, so many machine-made copies are being imported from other countries they don't have to work as hard. You have a better chance. I asked a collector-dealer how the dealers could get away with trying to sell a German or Chinese copy as an old Oriental. Her reply was that even the new rugs were handknotted. Therefore, they are classified as Orientals—since this is one of the techniques used on the authentic old rugs. So, if you don't know what you are doing, don't fool with Orientals. Sooner or later, as your knowledge and taste grow and improve, you'll find a beauty at a housesale that you can afford. The same expert also advises shoppers not to buy Orientals at auction. She claims it is a very "iffy" proposition since there isn't enough time to carefully examine the rugs. One bit of advice she did offer is to be sure the rug lies flat against the floor. A crumpled rug is one that may have shrunk, have a bad weave, or be otherwise damaged.

Hunter's Tip: Be sure to read a good Oriental rug book before looking at one at any kind of sale.

Certain objects that have been through their first vogue go up to astronomical prices when they are reproduced. They appear in their new form for equally Astronomical prices. Two such pieces are the French armoire and the brass-and-iron French bakery rack. While they certainly are handsome and practical pieces for any home, they are a "no-no." Unless you don't mind owning an expensive cliché. For a while every upper-middle-class, professionally decorated home had one or the other or both. Instead, what you want will be something different for storing your linens or holding your plants and objets d'art.

Storage pieces are always the most expensive and the hardest antiques to find. They are so practical. One of my friends grew tired of looking for a large cupboard or armoire. She went to an office supply house that offered oak cabinets for sale. She found a towering golden oak cabinet with dozens of drawers. Being a do-it-yourselfer, she and her husband created a storage wall out of it. Cheaper than hiring a carpenter these days. She had been hunting for many months for just the right piece to use as a storage wall. Another friend who couldn't find a beautiful armoire to serve as a bar opted instead for a pie safe with punched tin doors. It looks more Mexican than early American, and fits in with the contemporary living-room furnishings. A couple with several children and a new baby grew weary of high-priced tags on antique chests. At a country auction they bid on, and bought, a sturdy antique jelly cabinet. It holds baby needs, and needn't be junked when the nursery is later converted.

Hunter's Tip: Think imaginatively when hunting for storage pieces for your house. The end result will probably be cheaper and more effective than the commonly used pieces.

A kitchen of the 1930s had this type of stove and refrigerator. These doll-house appliances in metal copied the styles of the era. Pieces like these bring several dollars each at shops. These were found at a basement sale for a quarter each.

Sometimes it's wise to buy from dealers even though the price seems high. How often can you find a marquetry *poudreuse* like this one at any price? The interior is of birdseye maple. Legs have ebonized trim combined with marquetry in different shadings of wood. It is similar to Tunbridgeware pieces made in England and it dates from the middle of the nineteenth century. No clues appear since drawers aren't dovetailed and mirror is a replacement. Doubtless further research would trace the wood designs to a specific cabinetmaker.

For a long time I had been watching similar jewelry boxes going at auction for one hundred and fifty dollars and up. I felt lucky to find this at an antique shop for less. Especially since they are now going to dealers for even more money. The dealers then resell for additional markup because of the scarcity of authentic early nineteenth-century pieces.

Unusual leaded-glass windows are hard to find these days—even at antique shops. I found it hard to resist this one, with deep purple grapes and varying shades of green. It makes a perfect wine cellarette. Using the original brass hardware, a cabinet-maker built a cabinet around it to match existing kitchen cabinets. Should I move, it can easily be removed from its frame. I looked for the perfect window for almost a year before I discovered this one in a shop.

An elderly relative was going to put this hand carved oak pipe rack in the garbage. Then he remembered us. Would we be interested? The answer to my husband's pipe collection and a freebee. Consider, though, if he had tossed it, you might have seen it in your alley. One collector with a sharp eye found a sixteenth-century Spanish wayside shrine on top of a city ash-can—in full sight.

Lamps for the doll house copied the fashions of the times in which they were made. These were made in the 1930s. On the left is a "bridge lamp" in metal with a hand painted shade. On the right, a table lamp of silvery metal and, hand painted metal shade. Nickel and dime collectibles.

A unique pair of art nouveau brass andirons. Just what every fireplace needs. Especially when they are housesale priced at twelve dollars or less. The reason they were so inexpensively priced was probably because they didn't look like the usual colonial style. For some reason, nobody but me appreciated the animal feet and the outsize flower. The brass helmet scuttle, found at a collector's housesale, I thought fairly priced at twenty-five dollars—since it is a nineteenth-century piece in fairly good shape.

Old advertising paper dolls make a charming bit of art work in a child's room. These "children of the world" advertise Delicia butter. The entire set turned up at a housesale for a quarter.

Early handmade American quilts in poor condition can often be used in new guises. This popular early pattern in rose and pastel green can't be used as a bed cover. Why not cushions and pillows? Because of its worn appearance, it was purchased for four dollars. If it's good enough for interior decorators, it's good enough for you.

There is nothing like an old Navajo rug to dress up a floor or wall. These days you pay hundreds of dollars for similar rugs. Mine came from an unlikely housesale for under twenty dollars. I had been looking around for months for the right floor covering to go with my son's American primitive bedroom furnishings and rock-group posters. This was it—in bold designs and colors.

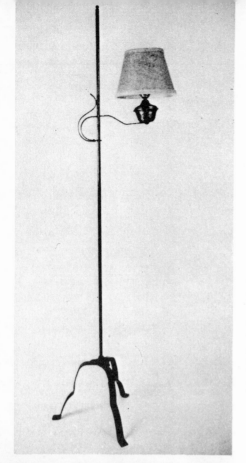

Decorators are rediscovering these 1920s versions of early American candle stands. These metal lamps were known as "bridge lamps" and were used at bridge games. The lamp part often adjusts up or down. They are perfect for rooms with early American decor. Posh antique dealers sell them for around a hundred dollars with a shade made from antique fabric. It's the shade, after all, that's an antique. You can find the lamps for three dollars in somebody's garage.

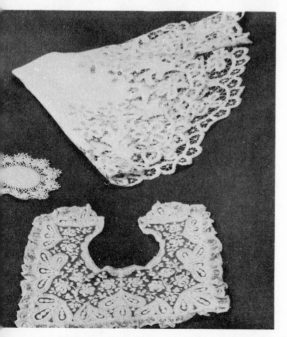

Bits and pieces of old lace are costly in shops, bargains in attic sales. Used in new ways, they add a touch of luxury to home furnishings.

This bamboo-turned Victorian easel was a garage-sale find. Instead of using a picture frame for large pieces of art work, they can be displayed on the easel and moved around. They can also make a decorative holder for handsome pieces of needlework.

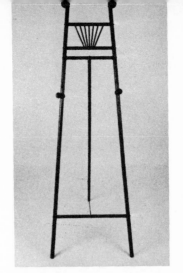

Unusual pieces of Victorian silver add elegance to even an informal party. The "fish set" (top) cost two dollars for a set of six at a garage sale. They are so oversized and gingerbready that they are fun to mix with different table settings. The silver shell dish was black when first seen—and budget priced. When polished, it can be used for Christmas cookies and petit fours.

Doll-house furniture often turns up at house and basement sales. This Windsor chair and desk were picked up for fifty cents each. They were handmade in Germany in the twenties and thirties. Today, if bought at shop prices, they bring much more.

16
Test Your Hunting Ability

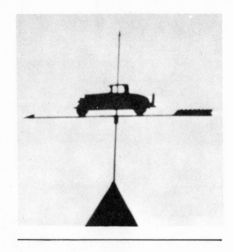

SEE HOW GOOD you are at psyching out antiques and collectibles—at least by their descriptions. If you get a fairly high score you have the markings of a successful hunter.

Case A: Oriental Rugs

You are hunting for Oriental rugs. Two ads that mention Chinese and Oriental rugs look promising. One sale is being held in a very expensive high-rise apartment, at a conducted estate sale. The other is a private sale of household furnishings.

1. Would you go first to the fancy estate sale? _____

2. Would you go at all to the other sale? _____

3. There are a dozen Orientals at the posh apartment sale. They are in bright deep blues and maroons, and in excellent condition. The seller points out that the owner kept everything in pristine condition. Should you consider a 9 x 12 for two thousand five hundred dollars? In a fine retail store you've seen the same type and name for five hundred more. _____

4. Before you write out a check you examine the back of the rug to see if it is loosely woven. This will prove whether it is a good or bad buy. _____

5. While examining the back you notice the pattern does not come through in the same way it does on the top. Should that bother you? _____

6. The seller tells you the rug is handknotted. Obviously, it is an antique. _____

7. You dampen a corner of your linen handkerchief and rub it against the colors. The blue and red come off on the cloth. Should you buy it anyhow? After all, don't old dyes tend to fade and rub off? _____

Answers

1. Yes—go but be a skeptic. Chances are it is a padded sale with new items brought in. However, it may be genuine. You'll never know if you don't go.

2. Yes. Providing you can beat the dealers through the sale doors. There is big money in antique

217

Orientals—so you must know the dealers will be beating down the doors. Try your luck.

3. Be suspicious of the colors if they seem garish. These could be some "hot off the assembly line" items being made in Italy and Iran. Hold on to your money for a few more minutes.

4. Not always. Be concerned with the beauty of design. Keep in mind some of the highly priced Turkish rugs are loosely woven. Learn all you can about Orientals of various kinds before you buy.

5. Yes. It is an important detail. On authentic Orientals the same pattern should be just as well done on the bottom as the top.

6. No. Even brand-new rugs are handknotted.

7. No. The final clue that tells you it is "new" is the fact that the dyes used are commercial—not vegetable—and rub off. The authentic Orientals, made by regional tribes, are dyed with natural colors—berries, bark, etc. They may also have a certain patina from being walked on by barefooted tribesmen. Try again.

Case B: Cut Glass

You are looking for glass knife rests to add to your collection—and a nice cut-glass bowl. You decide to visit the current visiting antique show. And, while you are at it you may find some tumblers to match your grandmother's water set.

1. Is the antique show worth the two dollar and fifty cents admission fee? _____

2. There are many glittering displays of cut glass. Much to your surprise there are some very interesting patterned knife rests. They are priced from twenty-five dollars each up. Should you buy one? ─────────

3. You spot a couple of sparkling glass bowls that you recognize as being in your favorite hobstar pattern. Taking out your magnifying glass you see the tiny lines of wear. The pattern is deeply cut and feels sharp to the touch. Does this mean it is new? ─────────

4. There is no signature, so it isn't worth the fifty-dollar price. ─────────

5. Tap it gently with your finger; it rings. Therefore, it is genuine, old cut glass. ─────────

Answers

1. Yes. Regardless of what you see or buy, every antique show is an education in itself. Consider you will be able to see how pricing is going up or down on various items. You can also check on local dealers who exhibit lots of reproductions, and remember to avoid them. You may also find some missing pieces to your silver or patterned glass. After all, when dealers come from all over the country you never know when one may have that missing item. You may also discover matching jewelry, or the proper arm for your broken doll.

2. No, if you haven't learned how to tag the many knife rests now being reproduced. Yes, if you find an authentic one. Twenty-five dollars is a reasonable price.

3. No. Give it a few more tests. Is it beautifully

polished? Does it seem quite heavy? New pieces are heavier. Remembering the look of the rims of the bowls you know to be old—compare. They will be cut slightly differently. Judge the pattern. Pinwheel, pineapple, fan, and feather are the most often reproduced.

4. No. It is a popular fallacy that a piece of glass must be signed to be worth anything at all. If the piece is beautifully cut, and you recognize it as authentic early cut glass, it is well worth the fifty dollars.

5. No. The "ring" only shows it is cut glass; not new pressed glass.

Case C: Oriental Lowestoft

At a very elegant antiques show you spot an American eagle plate and a bowl in the green Fitzhugh pattern. The dealer reminds you that this Chinese export porcelain is very rare and its already high price can only go up.

1. Would you instantly write out a check before another collector buys the pieces? _____

2. Examining the plate you give it a gentle thump with your finger. It answers you with a dull thud. This doesn't mean anything. _____ You test the bowl. It has a bell-like ring.

3. The bowl is heavier than the plate, and has a cold feel. This means it's authentic. _____

4. The dealer points out that there are no marks on either piece. This automatically certifies them as authentic. _____

Answers

1. No, a thousand times no. Instead you would be aware the Hong Kong artisans have been busy creating copies for the American tourist trade. You ask the dealer if you may examine the pieces very closely. There should be no objection.

2. The dull thud does mean you've found a reproduction. Real Lowestoft is a hard paste or true porcelain. When tapped it should give a bell-like ring, and have a translucency. The bowl is quite possibly true Lowestoft if it rings.

3. Yes—it is another clue to authenticity. Another clue would be trying to scratch the glaze with a steel knife. The authentic Lowestoft wouldn't scratch. Obviously the dealer isn't about to let you try that. So, you keep looking for other clues.

4. No. When the new pieces come into the United States they have either a paper or ink mark; Hong Kong or China, on the bottom. It doesn't take much effort to remove it. Presto! instant authentic Lowestoft. Buy the bowl. It has many characteristics of authenticity.

Case D: Welsh Cupboard

On viewing day at a very important auction you spot a beautiful Welsh cupboard in oak. There is nothing in the auction catalog to make you doubt its authenticity. You begin a careful examination to see if you should bid on it.

1. Opening the drawers, you notice they are hand-dovetailed and riddled with wormholes. These two facts mark its eighteenth-century origin.

2. The brasses are complete and beautifully wrought in the style of the period. Touching them with your handy-dandy magnet you discover they aren't really brass. Should you become suspicious? _____

3. Inside one of the drawers you spot the maker's label. Though worn, the piece is obviously marked and therefore an authentic piece. Hoping the dealers haven't noticed, you slide the drawer in place. Labels increase the value. _____

4. Pulling out another drawer you look underneath at the runners. They look brand-new. Is this important? _____

5. You look at the back for evidences of early woodworking tools. While the back is rough finish and dark you don't see the marks of the pit saw. Does this mean anything? _____

6. The top of the cupboard shows no warping. This is probably because the piece has been well-restored. _____

7. The patina has the look of antiquity. But it is in suspiciously good shape. Possibly this is merely due to it's being expertly restored. Besides, age marks and scars still show on the finish. _____

Answers

1. No. There are a couple of ways to fake wormholes. To test the holes, insert a small pin. It shouldn't go very far in a straight line. The worms aren't that precise—a drill is. The drawers might have been removed from another piece or they might be authentic. For the eighteenth century there

should only be one or two wide dovetails—not the same size.

2. No. Complete sets of brass hardware are a rarity. It is common for authentic antiques to have completely new hardware. Of course, if it were original this would be an important clue to authenticity.

3. No. Sorry but there are all kinds of ways to fake labels. You, too, can put an old label in your furniture. Find an old book, dating eighteenth century, remove an unprinted page, giving you the proper paper. Let a photoengraver make a cut of an authentic label, and have a printer add the proper touches. Let the label sit in a sunny window for a week or so. Don't let the label influence your decision. If it is important it will be so noted in the sale catalog. Labels up the price.

4. No. There is nothing unusual about replacement of runners when a piece is well restored.

5. Yes. The most important clue could be finding these early pitted saw marks. Of course, it is possible to add old boards to a new piece.

6. Yes and no. It is not a conclusive clue. There should be warping on anything three hundred years old. But, good restoration could set it right.

7. Yes. It is often hard to recognize the look of age on a well-restored piece. The thing that bothers you is that an awful lot of antique Welsh cupboards have been turning up and are very popular. You would do well not to bid, unless you get it very cheaply.

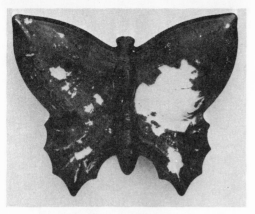

This pressed-glass butterfly is of a royal blue color. The paint is peeling off. Was this the work of an amateur who decided to paint it blue? Nope. This is Goofus glass. It was painted (before firing) in the late 1800s. It is fun to have a piece around—especially when you only paid a dime.

Another bottle mystery. Is it Mexican or early-nineteenth-century American? It was found at a garage sale for a quarter. Aqua in color. It stands ten inches high, has sixteen vertical ribs swirled to the left, a rough pontil, and a sheared lip. It has a clear, bell tone ring when tapped. The shape is unusual; it is best described as a decanter. Deductions resulting from research in McKearin's *American Glass* place it as early nineteenth century from a midwestern glassworks. Is it a rare Mantua, Ohio? Perhaps you can narrow the facts down still further.

This pitcher has no markings whatsoever on the bottom. It is pottery in the form of an ear of corn with yellow raised kernels and green leaves. Research tells you that it is a majolica syrup pitcher. Victorian vintage. It was found for a dollar at a garage sale.

This pear-shaped aqua bottle was a trade with some members of a bottle-collector's club. It is aqua in color with glass "quilling" on the sides. No rough pontil, no seams. No pictures in bottle books. Is it a phony? I finally discovered a similar bottle pictured in a book by George and Helen McKearin, *American Glass*. It is dated approximately 1775, English, free-blown with a tooled lip. The shape is known as a flattened ovoid. It was carried by travelers in their large coat pockets or sometimes covered by wicker. See what a little research does for you!

A late-nineteenth-century sampler found at a basement sale. The colors are so bright and fresh it looks new. There is no date embroidered on it. However, the seller noted that it had been wrapped up in a trunk for years; hence the almost new condition. Inspection under a good light showed some brown 'age spots—a good sign it wasn't done last week. Another clue to its age is the shape. Early samplers were oblong. Later Victorian ones were large squares.

It isn't always easy to tell at first glance what an object was used for. The lighting device on the left is a peg lamp. The small knob on the bottom fitted into the top of a candlestick. The added height gave better light. The sparking lamp on the right is easier to identify. It is made of pressed glass. They are fun to use, especially with colored and perfumed oil.

A nest of "quartetto" tables similar to those designed by Thomas Sheraton in 1803. The tops are veneered in a beautiful "oystering." They were purchased as English antiques at an estate sale. The tops have a patina. The legs and feet show little evidence of age—such as old nails or screws. One of the table bottoms has a number burned into the surface.

Deduction: The tops may possibly be old, but the bases are of a later date. The tables were probably imported from England in the 1920s. They are reproductions.

Sometimes old patterns are hard to track down. This one, with its shepherds and ornaments, should have a name like Christmas night. Finally found the pattern in a book called *Old China* by Minnie Watson Kamm. The pattern name is "Oriental." The first clue was the mark on the back—W. T. Copeland, Stoke On Trent, England. The fooler is that despite the word "England," usually identifying patterns dated after 1891, this one was done between 1847 and 1867. The colors are a cinnamon brown and white.

226

Appendix

Appendix:
Antique Hunting from A to Z

THERE IS ALWAYS something more to be said in the business of antiques and collectibles. Whether it is a new antique rarity that has just been discovered, a record sale at an auction house, or an up-and-coming freaky collectible that sends hunters combing the woodpiles. Putting the whole thing into an alphabetical perspective:

A is for authentic—be it antiques or collectibles. Such a piece should be of the proper date first—and in fine condition secondly. A general application for almost any piece is to check the object for (1) material it is made of. Even though it looks like brass or maple or old glass on the surface does it check out? (2) Does it have the proper design or motif of the period? If "Canton" or "Imari," are the figures or designs of Oriental or European influence? (3) Is it really from the country of origin it purports to be? An "Oriental" rug from Europe? A German stein from Japan? (4) Was the piece originally something else? Was the china cabinet once just a kitchen base cabinet from Sears Roebuck? Was the Chippendale chair always a chair or (5) was it altered? Like an original Chippendale leg and a chair built around it? (6) If furniture or other decorative art, are the tool marks proper for those of the period (circular saw marks, etc.)? (7) Is it an object that was actually in use at the period of history it seemingly fits into? (8) Is it the original finish? Are the "wear marks" recently made? (9) If it has papers of authenticity, can they be checked out?

B is for brasses—horse brasses. Doubtless you have seen them gleaming in shops abroad and your local antique dealers. Early and mid-Victorian brassfounders and saddlers' pattern books pictured over three hundred brasses to gussy up harnesses. The early brasses had designs identifying the owner's trade or area where he lived. From 1750 till the 1900s brasses were made for their original purpose. From the 1920s they were made as souvenirs, for decorations. Reproductions were made of the early brasses and aged to appear old. If you want the *old* pieces, become familiar with the patterns, look, and feel of that period. Before you buy in England, check your local gift shops to see how the new brasses look.

C is for clocks of all kinds that aren't as old as they look. Tall-case clocks with lunar dials are enjoying a revival. Those made late 1700s and early 1800s had dials with lunar and tidal faces made for a specific port. They usually are signed (1) at the lower edge of the hour ring, (2) across the bottom of the brass dial plate, or (3) on a separate plaque attached to the dial. Because most clock collectors are suspicious of an unsigned clock, *beware* of signatures of famous clockmakers. If possible, check the signature against a museum-piece signature. This "signature" is an engraving of the maker's name either in script or lettering. Many of the new tall-case clocks will have too much carving on the base of the case for the period. Be suspicious if the case is too fancy—Eastlake-type touches, etc.

D is for Depression glass. It was of the cheapest commercial quality, mass produced from 1920 to 1940. Many of the most decorative pieces attempted to use patterns from such earlier designs as Sandwich glass. Deep colors were used to cover up glass impurities. Everything from kitchenware to ash trays was made in this machine-molded glass. If you care, join one of the Depression-glass collectors clubs and learn the finer points.

E is for exhibits and the special catalogs or brochures documenting exhibit items. The major museums put together decorative arts exhibits several times a year. Objects are culled from private collections and a variety of sources. Their value to you lies in having rare examples of many objects in one place for reference. Catalogs are usually from five dollars up. Check various antiques publications for dates, costs, etc.

F is for freaky. What do you think about the current interest and high prices for Ku Klux Klan and Nazi mementos? This falls into the same category as collections of leg irons and prison gear. Then there are those who gleefully hang up Victorian coffin hardware as art objects. All fine for museums, but home sweet home?

F is also for firemarks. From the 1700s to mid-1800s firemarks were given to fire insurance policy holders. Made of wood, cast iron, tin or lead, they were placed on the front of buildings to show the volunteer firemen you were entitled to protection. It also indicated the firemen would be paid should they save *that* building. Their designs were whimsical renderings of firemen, engines and hoses, trees, etc. Reproductions are rampant.

G is for gadgets. Call it kitsch or collectibles, kitchen gadgets by the hundreds were patented in the 1920s. Eggbeaters, revolving cookie cutters and all kinds of kitchen helpers evolved along with the gas range. Which just goes to show eventually anything becomes a collectible. It all depends on how often you clean out the basement: who knows what may be tomorrow's gem!

H is for hardware. If you are refinishing or trying to make an antique as authentic as possible, the proper hardware is a must. Check the advertising pages of antique trade publications for "hardware reproductions." Or, check your local hardware store. Probably less expensive than buying the knobs, H-hinges, etc. at the antique shows. Even the fruit and floral Vic-

torian carved drawer pulls can be found this way—
new, of course.

I is for iron doorstop, made from 1890 to the 1930s.
They are one of the *least expensive* antiques or collectibles around. And, still plentiful. Look next to the
door at housesales—where else? Pay from two to
ten dollars. Shaped like animals, people, and ships.

J is for Japanning. In the eighteenth and nineteenth
centuries wood and metals were covered with varnish,
paint and gilt imitating Japanese lacquer techniques.

K is for knotted pine. Though popular it isn't a mark
of an antique piece of furniture—at least not unless
the piece formerly was painted. If so, it should be a
rough knot.

L is for leaded glass. Also called flint glass. Its content
of lead oxide determines whether or not the glass
will ring "like a bell" when tapped. A test for old,
supposed flint glass is to tap for a ring.

M is for music boxes of all types. They always command top prices and are probably one of the hardest
antiques to find at modest prices. A fine Swiss-made
music box with several instruments and its own table
will go at auction for a couple of thousand dollars.
Consider a recording of old music boxes if the effect
is what you seek.

N is for Nippon porcelain, exported to the United States
from Japan into the early 1900s. Before World War I,
the Japanese referred to their country as Nippon—
the Chinese word for "sun origin." Master copiers

that they are, Nippon porcelain may resemble Limoges, Royal Bayreuth, and Wedgwood. While it is still relatively inexpensive in metropolitan areas, it goes over big in small towns—and the prices are up. Much is handpainted.

O is for oddities that people collect, like oilers. While a collection of old oil cans can turn your parlor into a garage, consider what Occupied Japan figurines of dime-store pottery would do? If you must collect something beginning with "O" try opaline glassware, or ormolu.

P is for prints—originals, not restrikes. Sporting prints by Henry Alken; aquatints by French artists turn up at garage and rummage sales. Examine closely and try for those with plate marks. (Plate marks are the indentation made by the edges of the plate on the print. It forms the frame of an etching or line-engraving. If the plate mark is cut off it is hard to tell a new print that has been aged, from an original.

Q is for Quimper pottery. The early pieces were made in France beginning in the eighteenth century. What you'll find was made in the twentieth century. Because of the quaint folk-figure designs many buyers think it is earlier than it is. It is overpriced.

R is for railroad collectibles. Everything from old timetables to date nails and silver used on trains has a price tag. Early prints are among the most expensive items in this category. Let your taste be your guide.

S is for sheet music, especially when famous name personalities are pictured on the cover—or it is a first edition by a famous composer? Consider collecting music of a special theme. One collector in the tea-and-coffee business collects only sheet music with these two subjects. While your collection may not be worth millions it will be great for conversation—and entertainment.

T is for trade catalogs—the earlier the better. So popular that many like Sears have been reprinted. Toy, glass, and silver collectors find them a valuable reference to what pieces they should look for to add to collections. Basements and rummage sales are good places to look.

U is for upholstery. To have your upholstered pieces done in the proper period motif, check the textile departments of your local museum. If you can't find current reproductions at least you can find similar designs. Several fabric houses specialize in reproducing early designs—among them Brunschwig & Fils. While early designs from abroad (pre-Revolution) featured traditional nature and floral motifs, after the Revolution, Washington, the Revolution, and other historical designs were used. From then on history was part of fabric designs till after the Civil War.

V is for violins—and all the violins that keep turning up with Stradivarius labels. The original Stradivarius label read, "Antonius Stradivarius Cremonensis Faciebat Anno 1714." So does a fake Stradivarius. These phony violins were sold from the 1880s till the early 1900s. According to experts, all of the known Stradivarius violins are recorded. Equally popular are phony Guarnerius labels. If there is another name inside your violin it may be of value. Check with a reputable violin teacher or the library for names of violin makers.

W is for wicker furniture that was made in the 1920s. It is making its way out of attics and to the sales. At auctions it is often bid up out of proportion to its value. It isn't *that* old. Early wicker was made from the 1850s on. By the end of the nineteenth century it was ornate. Today it is expensive when in good condition. Try and find the plainer style of the twenties before the dealers do. Lamp shades and floor lamps, tables, chairs and plant holders are possibilities.

W is also for Windsor chairs. Author-artist Wallace Nutting said all there is to say about Windsor chairs in his Furniture Treasury books. Windsors have been and are still being reproduced. Many from the 1920s by now must look positively ancient. What you want are those made prior to 1800. Second choice will be those made in the Victorian era. The more spindles the older the Windsor. The Windsor came to America from England around 1725. The first American Windsors were the low-backs. Today we call them either firehouse or captain's chairs. They were followed by the comb-backs. Studying the variations and history of the Windsor can be a specialty in itself. Nine spindles are fine; from eleven to thirteen even better —and important. Children's chairs can still be found using the Windsor design.

W is also for woodcarvings—toys, sculpture, and other classified American folk art. Once considered primitive, nineteenth-century and earlier examples of hand-carving are being eagerly collected. Here is one current collectible that makes sense—and can only increase in value. Again, let your good taste be your guide. Ugly and poorly done, it is always just that—regardless of age.

X is for Xerox machines—a boon to you when you need a copy of a book page or illustration—and can't afford the book. Most public libraries have a photocopy machine of some sort. Use it to record information about the things you collect—auction prices, discoveries, or general news. Usually ten cents a page. Good when you can't remove certain books from the library.

Y is for yokes—the type used by farmers. Pick them up for from fifty cents to two dollars. Sand the hand-carved wood; remove rust from the iron or brass rings. Presto! the best-looking antique towel holder you've ever seen.

Z is for Zeppelin—especially first-flight covers of the Graf Zeppelin dated to 1929—and postcards of the Hindenburg Zeppelin. Something for specialist collectors to add to their airpline flying-machine collections.